D1502458

BORED
GAMES

BORED GAMES

100+ In-Person and Online Games to Keep Everyone Entertained

Adams Media

New York   London   Toronto   Sydney   New Delhi

Adams Media
An Imprint of Simon &
Schuster, Inc.
57 Littlefield Street
Avon, Massachusetts 02322

Copyright © 2021 by
Simon & Schuster, Inc.

All rights reserved, including
the right to reproduce this book
or portions thereof in any form
whatsoever. For information
address Adams Media Subsidiary
Rights Department, 1230 Avenue of
the Americas, New York, NY
10020.

First Adams Media hardcover
edition January 2021

ADAMS MEDIA and colophon are
trademarks of Simon & Schuster.

For information about special
discounts for bulk purchases, please
contact Simon & Schuster Special
Sales at 1-866-506-1949 or
business@simonandschuster.com.

The Simon & Schuster Speakers
Bureau can bring authors to your
live event. For more information or
to book an event contact the Simon
& Schuster Speakers Bureau at
1-866-248-3049 or visit our website
at www.simonspeakers.com.

Interior design by
Colleen Cunningham
Interior illustrations by
Priscilla Yuen

Manufactured in the United States
of America

10 9 8 7 6 5 4 3 2 1

Library of Congress Cataloging-in-
Publication Data
Names: Adams Media (firm).
Title: Bored games.
Description: Avon, Massachusetts:
Adams Media, 2021. | Includes
index.
Identifiers: LCCN 2020008735 |
ISBN 9781507214039 (hc) | ISBN
9781507214046 (ebook)
Subjects: LCSH: Games. |
Entertaining.
Classification: LCC GV1229 .B494
2020 | DDC 793--dc23
LC record available at https://lccn
.loc.gov/2020008735

ISBN 978-1-5072-1403-9
ISBN 978-1-5072-1404-6 (ebook)

Many of the designations used
by manufacturers and sellers to
distinguish their products are
claimed as trademarks. Where
those designations appear in this
book and Simon & Schuster, Inc.,
was aware of a trademark claim,
the designations have been printed
with initial capital letters.

Contains material adapted from
the following title published by
Adams Media, an Imprint of Simon
& Schuster, Inc.: *The Everything®
Big Book of Party Games* by Carrie
Sever, copyright © 2014, ISBN
978-1-4405-7295-1.

Contents

Introduction 11

The Games 13
1920s Dance-Off 15
ABC Roundup 17
All Thumbs 18
Apple on a String 19
Artist's Paint-and-Pass 20
Ask Me About… 22
Back-to-Back 23
Back-to-Back Balloon Dash 25
Back-to-Back Sumo 26
Ball Battle 27
Balloon Keep-Away 28
Balloon Waddle 29
Balloon Word Scramble 30
Blind Man's Treasure 32
Bobble Head 33
Bridge Master 35
Bucket Guard 36
Caddy Stack 38
Candy Hunt 39
Candy Relay 40

Carrot Toss... 41

Celebrity Dinner Theater 42

Celebrity Hunt 43

Chalky Target 45

Check Your Pockets 46

Cheese Taste-Off 47

Clipboard Tennis 48

Commercial Life.. 49

Cookie Face 50

Crystal Clear Game....................................... 51

Cups and Downs 52

Defy Gravity 53

Don't Look Back.. 54

Dress-and-Dash Relay 56

Dress-Off 57

Drop, Sink, and Clink 59

Egg Drop.. 60

Egg Head Spin-and-Attack................................. 61

Egg Roller Relay... 62

Feed Me! 64

Fishbowl 65

Flip-a-Song Karaoke 66

Flip-Book Frenzy 67

Flour Game 69

Following the Leader 70

Fragile-Package Toss 71

Freeze.. 72

Going on a Picnic.. 73

Grand Tour.. 74

Guess That Tune 75

Gum Bobbing 76

Head Pendulum 77

Hide-and-Seek 78

Homemade Ball Toss 80

Hoop Toss.. 81

Horse 82

Household Scavenger Hunt....................................... 83

How's Yours?... 84

Hungry Puzzler... 85

Hurry! Hurry! Make the List 86

Improv in a Bag 87

Ingredients Throw-Down 88

Job Charades 89

Jug Master... 91

Leap Spoon... 92

Mad Lib Story 93

Masquerade.. 95

Minute-to-Win-It Iron Man 96

Model Drawing... 97

Monkey See, Monkey Do.. 98

Most Likely To.. 99

Movie and Show Trivia 100

Movie Trivia... 101

Mug Shots 102

Mummy Wrap... 105

Murder Mystery Game... 106

Musical Balance... 108

Musical Teacups... 110

Name the Celebrity.. 111

Name the Difference... 112

Never Have I Ever 113

Nickname Name Tag 115

Noodling Around... 116

Office Chair Catapult.. 117

Office Supply Fishing.. 118

On Your Mark, Get Set, Draw!................................... 120

Ostrich Dance.. 121

Our Future and Then... 122

Paper Scraper 123

Pass the Mango 125

Pin the Mullet on the Dude 126

Plastic Wrap 128

Prediction Bingo 129

Presentation Memory.. 130

Psychologist 131

Puff Ball Fight.. 132

Room Recall... 133

Rorschach Test 134

Shakedown.. 135

Shoes Up 137

Slippery Dash 138

Sneak a Peek 139

Song Charades 140

Soul Mate 141

Spice Savvy 142

Spoon Brainteaser.. 144

Spoons.. 145

Stack Me 147

Steal the Bacon 148

Sticky Famous 149

Stuff the Sock 150

Tabletop Pyramid 152

Take a Hike! 153

Talent Search 154

Tea Party 155

Tennis Balls in the Balance 157

Trash Can Basketball 158

Truth or Dare 159

Truth or Manners 160

Try to Guess Celebrity Guests 161

Turkey Feather Blow 162

Tweezed 164

Two Truths and a Lie 165

'Ulu Maika 166

Uphill Battle 167

Volcano 168

Volleyball Splash 169

Water Balloon Hunt 170

Water Balloon Scramble 171

Watermelon Ninja 173

What's That Line? 174

Appendix: Games by Type 175

Index 181

Introduction

As the saying goes, "If you're bored, then you're boring"—so stop being boring and start having fun! With more than one hundred entertaining games to play, *Bored Games* provides hours upon hours of friendly competition and tons of fun.

No party? No problem! These games are perfect to play with spouses, kids, siblings, roommates, close friends, or anyone you're comfortable competing against. There are also ways to modify certain games so they can be played on your preferred video conferencing platform. Just because you can't meet up in person doesn't mean you can't enjoy each other's company!

Outdoors, indoors, at home, or on the go—there's a game in here that's right for you. For easy reference, the games are arranged alphabetically, and each one gives you information on how many players are required and what you need to play (if anything). And at the end of the book is a list of the games divided by category (summer games, scavenger hunts, etc.), so you can find what you're looking for quickly and easily.

So get ready to bare your soul (or not!) in Truth or Dare, get competitive with the Flour Game, or test your musical knowledge with What's That Line? It's time to put an end to boredom and start having fun!

The Games

1920s Dance-Off

Change up your after-dinner routine by throwing a 1920s dance-off. Give everyone a choice of the following dances to learn and compete with: the fox-trot, the turkey trot, the Charleston, and the black bottom. When dinner is finished, invite everyone to compete in the dance-off. Those who are not participating will be the judges. This game is even cooler if everyone dresses up in 1920s style.

NUMBER OF PLAYERS

4 or more

WHAT YOU'LL NEED

1920s music

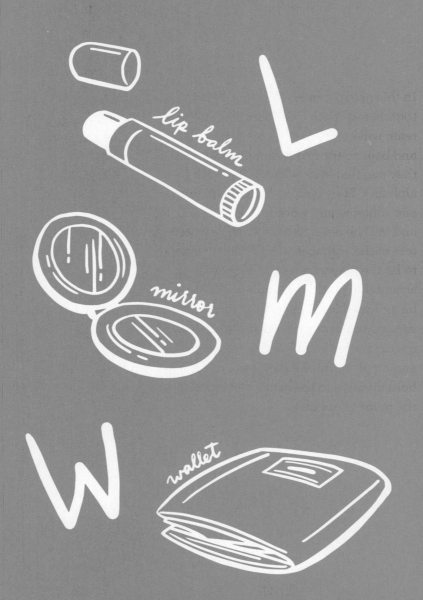

lip balm

mirror

wallet

ABC Roundup

In this group game, teammates work together to reach a collective goal. Each team will empty their pockets, purses, and bags to try to get as many items as they can that start with a letter in the alphabet. For example, lip balm, mirror, and wallet would work for the letters L, M, and W. The team to collect the most letters of the alphabet wins. You can choose to let the players allow brand names as acceptable points, but only one letter can be assigned for each item. If you want to expand the game, invite additional players to join via your favorite video conferencing platform. All they have to do is hold the item to the camera in order for the point to count.

NUMBER OF PLAYERS

4 or more (at least 2 groups of 2)

WHAT YOU'LL NEED

N/A

All Thumbs

This game can go on during dinner and continue for the rest of the night if so desired. Tell everyone the basic rules of the game. At the beginning of dinner, you will secretly assign someone to be the person who is "all thumbs." This person will choose a time during dinner to place both of his or her thumbs on the table, but will not say anything and just wait for others to notice. When someone notices it, that person must place his or her thumbs on the table as well.

This continues until there is only one person who hasn't noticed. You can choose to have this person do something funny for losing, reveal something special about him- or herself, or just have him or her start the next round. This game will have everyone really trying to pay attention, and they are sure to laugh it up as it takes others a while to catch on.

NUMBER OF PLAYERS

4 or more

WHAT YOU'LL NEED

N/A

Apple on a String

Lean the board up against a tree or wall, secured so it will not fall, with the nail pointed outward. Tie the string around the apple to secure it, with enough string left over that you are able to swing the apple. Each person will line up to swing the apple at the board, trying to get the apple to hit the nail and stay put. Each player gets three tries, and then it is the next person's turn. You can do rounds and give points for success. After three rounds of three tries for each player, whoever has the most points wins. Due to the nail involved in the game, make certain all of the players are positioned away from the board at a safe distance, and that the board is firmly in place at all times. Make sure you dispose of the board safely when the game is finished.

NUMBER OF PLAYERS

2 or more

WHAT YOU'LL NEED

Board with nail hammered through

String

Apple

Artist's Paint-and-Pass

Have everyone gather around a table. Place the sheet of paper in front of one of the painters and put the paints in the middle of the table with the brushes. Artists will paint whatever they like on the paper for one minute and then pass it to the left. The paper will continue around the table until everyone has a turn. There's not a winner to this game; instead, you all get to admire the contribution you made to the work of art. The more people play this game, the more creative the artwork will get.

3 or more

Large piece of paper

Paints

Brushes

Ask Me About...

On a bunch of name tags (as many as there are people in the house, or joining your next Zoom party), write conversation icebreakers. For instance:

○ Worst date I ever had
○ Strangest meal I ever ate
○ Weirdest thing ever said to me
○ Longest unexpected trip I ever took

As people arrive, in person or virtually, have the host assign a name tag to everyone. Then, at some point in the evening, someone can ask each person what the answer to his or her question is. At the end, when everyone has answered, vote on the winner for the best story.

NUMBER OF PLAYERS

4 or more

WHAT YOU'LL NEED

Stick-on name tags

Back-to-Back

Have two players sit on the floor, back-to-back. The object is to try to stand up without the use of your hands. It requires everyone to work to stand together. With each successful stand-up, add someone else to join the first two players. Continue until the group can no longer stand as a whole. Challenge your friends by sending videos of your group's attempts—see if they can do any better.

NUMBER OF PLAYERS

2 or more

WHAT YOU'LL NEED

N/A

Back-to-Back Balloon Dash

Water balloons are great on a summer day. Playing a game where you try not to pop one may sound odd, but it is very funny to watch. Set a point for the start of the race and for the finish line. Have the players split up into teams of two and hand out one water balloon to each team. The object of the game is to have the players stand back-to-back and place a water balloon between their backs. They must make it to the designated finish line without popping their balloon in order to win. If the balloon pops, then they have to start all over again. Due to the use of balloons, before the game ask each player if he or she is allergic to latex. You may need to avoid playing this game and other games involving balloons/latex.

NUMBER OF PLAYERS

4 or more

WHAT YOU'LL NEED

Latex water balloons

Back-to-Back Sumo

Sumo wrestling can be quite entertaining to watch, so why not host a match of your own? With variations, of course, this game can make for good laughs. Place a sheet of newspaper, spread out, on the ground. Two people, the sumo wrestlers, will stand back-to-back, shoulders touching, on top of the newspaper. Next, with their backs continuously against each other, they have to try to push each other off the newspaper. The first person to step off or to lose contact with the other person's back is out, and someone new comes in to try. The person who wins the round gets a point each time. This continues until everyone has tried. The sumo with the most points at the end wins the game.

NUMBER OF PLAYERS

2 or more

WHAT YOU'LL NEED

Sheets of newspaper

Ball Battle

Each person will receive a spoon and a ball. Players place the ball on the spoon, holding the spoon in one hand only. The object of the game is to keep the ball on the spoon while attempting to knock your opponents' tennis balls off their spoons by any means possible. All the players will be scrambling to keep their ball and spoon safe. The last person with the ball still on his or her spoon wins the game.

3 or more

2 large kitchen spoons

2 tennis balls

Balloon Keep-Away

This game will keep the players on their toes at all times. Set the stopwatch to two minutes. Each player will have an air-filled balloon tied to his or her ankle. The mission is to not only try to pop the other teams' balloons but to also protect your own. Once the time is up, the team with the most balloons left wins the game. Due to the use of balloons, make sure no one is allergic to latex before the game.

NUMBER OF PLAYERS

4 or more divided into teams of 2 or more

WHAT YOU'LL NEED

Stopwatch

Latex balloons

String

Balloon Waddle

To begin this game, you need to supply each player with an air-filled balloon. You also need to map out a race area that is at least twenty feet in distance, and mark a finish line. The object of the game is for each person to place the balloon between his or her knees and hurry to cross the finish line. The first person to reach the finish line without dropping the balloon or causing it to pop becomes the winner. Players who drop their balloon must turn around and start over. If the players pop the balloon, they must go back for a new one and start over. Due to the use of balloons, ensure no one is allergic to latex before the game.

NUMBER OF PLAYERS

2 or more

WHAT YOU'LL NEED

Latex balloons

Balloon Word Scramble

To get this game going, inflate the balloons, and write a letter on each balloon with the marker. For the vowels, you'll want to do several of each, and make more balloons with the letters D, M, N, R, S, and T. When all of the balloons are prepared, scatter them on the floor and separate your guests into two teams.

Each person or team, if you're playing in groups, will run in and pick six random balloons and go back to their area. They now have three minutes to come up with as many words as they can, using the letters they picked. For each word they make, they receive one point. At the end of the three minutes, they must show their words to each other to verify them and tally their points with the pencil and paper. They do three rounds. Whoever has accumulated the most points by the end of the game wins. Due to the use of balloons, make sure no player is allergic to latex before the game.

Blind Man's Treasure

Have everyone partner up. One of the partners is to be blindfolded. The host of the game will choose a prize, and once the players have their blindfold on, he or she will put the prize somewhere in the room. When the host says, "Go," the blindfolded partners will be directed to it by their seeing partners. The seeing partners cannot leave the spot they are in; they can only give verbal commands. Set the stopwatch for one minute. Whoever secures the object before the time is up gets a point for his or her team. After several rounds of this game, tally the points and see which team wins. Be careful of safety concerns and remove easily breakable objects from the playing area.

NUMBER OF PLAYERS

4 or more divided into teams

WHAT YOU'LL NEED

Blindfold

Small objects

Stopwatch

Bobble Head

A player straps the pedometer headband
onto his or her head and makes sure that
it is set to zero. The timer should be set to
one minute. When it starts, the player will
need to move his or her head and body
to get the pedometer to start registering
steps. If the headband starts to slip off,
players can fix it but must keep going.
If someone reaches 125 steps in one minute, that person wins this game. If no one
reaches it, the person with the highest
step count at the end of a minute wins.
This is a fun one to play on your favorite
video conference platform. Turn those
talking-head squares into bobble-head
squares!

NUMBER OF PLAYERS

3 or more

WHAT YOU'LL NEED

Pedometer clamped
to a headband

Timer

Bridge Master

Fill each bag with the same pieces and amounts of building blocks. Give a bag to each player, then have the players sit apart from one another so their pieces don't get mixed up and they don't copy anyone. Tell them that they have five minutes to use their pieces to build a sturdy bridge. After the five minutes are up, you will use the egg to test out whether the bridge can handle the weight of it. The player whose bridge stays intact with the egg on it wins. You can also square off against other friends or households by sending videos of your bridge building to see who can build the stronger bridge. (Just make sure you all have the same set of blocks!)

NUMBER OF PLAYERS

3 or more

WHAT YOU'LL NEED

Brown paper lunch bags

Plastic building blocks

Hard-boiled medium-sized egg

Bucket Guard

This game is played outside. Have the players split up into two teams. One team will be the bucket guards, and the other team will be the infiltrators. The object of the game is for the infiltrators to get as many water balloons or balls into the buckets while the bucket guards are swinging the bats to try to keep them out of the buckets.

Hand each bucket guard a bat and a bucket to set at his or her feet. Next, place a large tub of water balloons or balls behind the infiltrators. The infiltrators must stand at least eight to ten feet from the buckets. When someone yells, "Go," the players will begin tossing or guarding, depending on which team they are on. The players can throw their balloons at any of the buckets. At the end of three minutes, stop and count the number of balloons in each bucket. The team to get the most balloons or balls into the buckets wins (a balloon doesn't count if it breaks in the bucket). For the next round, empty the balloons (and water) out of the buckets, and have the guards switch places with the infiltrators. Due to the use of balloons, make sure no player is allergic to latex before the game.

4 or more

Plastic or foam baseball bat

Buckets (enough for each bucket guard)

Tub for water balloons

Latex water balloons or plastic balls in 2 different colors

Caddy Stack

Place the three golf balls on a flat surface. When the clock starts, players will have to stack the golf balls one on top of the other. Whoever can get all three of the balls stacked and staying that way for the longest time (at least three seconds) wins.

NUMBER OF PLAYERS

2 or more

WHAT YOU'LL NEED

3 golf balls

Stopwatch

Candy Hunt

Everyone knows that finding sweet treats is the best. And this is a great way to sweeten any in-person or virtual get-together. Call out a slogan associated with the candy. The first person to call out the right candy name gets rewarded with a piece of the candy. Here is the slogan list:

NUMBER OF PLAYERS

4 or more

WHAT YOU'LL NEED

Candy from following list

SLOGAN	CANDY NAME
Taste the rainbow	Skittles
Sometimes you feel like a nut, sometimes you don't	Almond Joy and Mounds
It's all in the mix; or Need a moment?	Twix
Get the sensation	YORK Peppermint Pattie
Gimme a break	Kit Kat
Melts in your mouth, not in your hand	M&M's
How many licks does it take to get to the center...?	Tootsie Pops
Isn't life juicy?	Starburst
A lighter way to enjoy chocolate	3 Musketeers
First they're sour, then they're sweet	Sour Patch Kids
There's no wrong way to eat a...	Reese's Peanut Butter Cups
Don't let hunger happen to you	Snickers
At work, rest, or play you get three great tastes with a...	Milky Way
Nobody's gonna lay a finger on my...	Butterfinger

Candy Relay

Place a cup and straw in front of each participant. Pour the candy in the bowl and place the bowl on the other side of the room on a table. The object of the game is for participants to use the straw to suck up a piece of candy and keep it on the straw long enough to bring it across the room to their cup and drop it in. The person with the most candies in his or her cup at the end wins the game.

NUMBER OF PLAYERS

4 or more

WHAT YOU'LL NEED

Plastic cups

Paper drinking straws without the bend in them

Candies such as Skittles or M&M's

Large bowl for candy

Carrot Toss

Begin by laying the Hula-Hoops in a row four or five feet apart from one another. Split into teams or pairs and give each team a bunch of carrots. The game starts with one person from each team standing about six feet from the row of Hula-Hoops. Each player must toss his or her carrot and try to land it inside one of the hoops.

When a player misses, the next person will go but must take a step back before tossing. If that person makes the toss, he or she receives a point for the team and the next person goes. After everyone has tossed once or twice, the team with the most points wins the game.

NUMBER OF PLAYERS

4 divided into teams

WHAT YOU'LL NEED

Hula-Hoops

Carrots

Celebrity Dinner Theater

Before dinner, write down on a piece of paper the names of several celebrities with whom most people would be familiar. Place one name under each person's plate before everyone sits down to eat. Once everyone is done eating, have them look under their plate and read the name silently. They now have to carry on like that celebrity, without acknowledging who they are, until someone can guess who they are. They can even act out some of the roles the celebrity has played or things the celebrity is famous for. The person to guess the most correct celebrities wins the game.

NUMBER OF PLAYERS

4 or more

WHAT YOU'LL NEED

Paper

Pen

Celebrity Hunt

The trick with this game is to make it *fast*. Sit in a circle or launch a virtual hangout and choose one person to go first. Everyone else shouts, "Hunt!" Immediately, the chosen person names a celebrity. Next, everyone shouts, "Hunt!" again. The next person in the circle must name another celebrity whose first name begins with the last letter of the previous celebrity's last name (it's permissible to use one-name celebrities such as Adele or Cher). Anyone who hesitates or can't come up with a name has to drop out until there's only one person left.

NUMBER OF PLAYERS

4 or more

WHAT YOU'LL NEED

N/A

Chalky Target

With chalk draw a large target on a concrete surface. Inside the center ring of the target, draw a 3 for three points; in the next ring, draw a 2 for two points, and in the outer ring, put the number 1 for one point. Put the bucket next to the starting line, which should be about six feet away from the target. Place the sponges in the bucket of water to let them soak.

Have the players line up and grab a sponge from the bucket, and then have them toss the sponge toward the target to see how many points they can hit. Have them rotate around so they can try at least two times. If you have a small group, you might let them try at least three times. The one with the most points at the end is the winner.

NUMBER OF PLAYERS

4 or more

WHAT YOU'LL NEED

Chalk

Bucket filled with water

Kitchen sponges

Check Your Pockets

This game only requires someone to call out random objects to the group of guests, whether it's in person or online in a virtual hangout. The caller will call out a random item, like lipstick. The first person to hold up the item receives the points for it. The person with the most points at the end wins the game.

NUMBER OF PLAYERS

6 or more

WHAT YOU'LL NEED

N/A

Cheese Taste-Off

Set up by laying out the cheese and placing a number in front of each one. You will need a master list for yourself with the name of each cheese on it. Have water and crackers laid out so that everyone can clean their palates after each tasting.

When everyone is ready, give them pen and paper and have them go down the line, sampling each cheese and guessing what cheese it is. This game takes care of an appetizer and entertainment. Once they have all sampled the cheeses and completed the cheese-guessing list, you can see who guessed the most correctly. Note that you'll want to check with everyone for food allergies beforehand. For vegans, make sure to use a vegan cheese substitute.

NUMBER OF PLAYERS

2 or more

WHAT YOU'LL NEED

Several flavors of cheese

Glasses of water

Plain salt-free crackers

Pens

Paper

Clipboard Tennis

Wad up some paper balls and have players stand about fifteen feet from a wastebasket. Have someone toss some paper wads at a player, who will use the clipboard to hit them into the trash can. The player must get two in before the one-minute mark is up.

4 or more

Crumpled-up paper

Trash can

Clipboard

Stopwatch

Commercial Life

This is a great game to play either in person or with a large group on your favorite video conferencing platform. Everyone must pick any simple item from around the home or office and create a commercial for it. They will have fifteen minutes to get the commercial ready, and then they will present it to the group. Everyone then votes as to whether or not they would buy the product based on the commercial. The one with the most potential sales wins.

NUMBER OF PLAYERS

4 or more

WHAT YOU'LL NEED

Index cards

Cookie Face

The goal of this game is very simple. A player leans his or her head back while another player puts a cookie on his or her forehead. The object of the game is to get the cookie from the forehead into the mouth without players using their hands. Whoever can do it in under one minute wins the game.

NUMBER OF PLAYERS

2 or more

WHAT YOU'LL NEED

Cookies

Stopwatch

Crystal Clear Game

Fill three of the glasses half full with water. Line up all six glasses in a row, alternating the half-full and empty glasses so that the even glasses are empty and the odd glasses are half full. The trick is to figure out how to move just one glass to make it so that three of the glasses with water are next to one another, and the three empty glasses are in a row together. Let everyone try to figure out what they would need to do to make this happen.

The answer is to pick up the fifth glass, pour the liquid into the second glass, and set the empty glass back down in the fifth spot. The first three glasses are now full, and the last three are empty—goal accomplished. This one is good to do with one to two people at a time, so that if anyone gets it, few hear the answer and others can have a shot at trying it.

Cups and Downs

Have players separate into two teams. One team will be the Ups and one team will be the Downs. Place around forty cups in the middle of the room, half of them facing up and half of them facing down. Have the Ups team stand in front of the cups facing down, and have the Downs team stand in front of the cups facing up. Set the timer for one minute and notify the teams that they have one minute to flip the cups to face the opposite direction. The team that has the most cups flipped at the end of the timer wins. (You can make it easier on the judge by having the Ups' cups one color and the Downs' cups another.)

4 or more divided into 2 teams

Plastic cups

Timer

Defy Gravity

Give each player two air-filled balloons. Using only their hands, they must keep the balloons in the air and off the floor for one minute. If anyone drops a balloon, she or he is out. If two or more of the players have successfully kept their balloons in flight, increase to three balloons for the next round. Keep going, increasing one balloon each round until only one person is left. Due to the use of balloons, before the game ask if anyone is allergic to latex.

NUMBER OF PLAYERS

2 or more

WHAT YOU'LL NEED

Latex balloons

Stopwatch

Don't Look Back

One player from each team stands in front of her or his team member, back facing the person. The person from behind tosses puff balls, one at a time, over the head of the other team member, who must catch them in the party hat. Teams take turns of five balls each. The first team to catch a total of five balls wins the game.

NUMBER OF PLAYERS

4 or more divided into teams

WHAT YOU'LL NEED

Puff balls

A cone-shaped party hat

Dress-and-Dash Relay

Put a bunch of vintage clothing items on one side of the room and have everyone stand on the other. Have the players split into teams. The first team will step up, and when the timer starts, one player will run across the room and put all the items on as fast as he or she can. That person will then run to his or her team, touch hands with a member of the team, and run back to where you've placed the clothes and quickly get undressed. Once that person returns to the team, the next player does the same thing. This continues until every player has had a turn or until the timer stops. The next team will take its turn and try to beat the previous team's time. The team with the best time wins the challenge.

NUMBER OF PLAYERS

4 or more

WHAT YOU'LL NEED

Leisure suit

Wigs

Platform shoes

Timer

Dress-Off

Start by placing all of the clothing items in the bag and set up the music. Have everyone gather around in a circle, and hand the bag to one of the players. When the music starts, the players start to pass around the bag. When the music stops, the player holding the bag closes his or her eyes and reaches in to grab one item and puts it on. Once the music starts back up, the passing around of the bag continues. This will go on until all the items are taken. One person will act as the judge, decide which of the outfits is best, and pick the winner of the contest.

4 or more

Assortment of wearable items (shirts, hats, beads, buttons, wigs, pants, socks)

Garbage bag

Music

Drop, Sink, and Clink

Fill the fishbowls up about 75 percent of the way with water and put a shot glass in the middle of each one, then place the fishbowls on the floor in a row. When the game starts, each player will need to grab one quarter at a time and drop it into the shot glass inside the bowl. The player must drop the quarter from three feet up. If he or she can make the quarter into all three shot glasses, that person wins the game. If the number of players is divisible by three, divide into teams.

NUMBER OF PLAYERS

3 or more

WHAT YOU'LL NEED

Water

3 (2-gallon) fishbowls

3 shot glasses

A cup of quarters

Egg Drop

First, separate the players into teams, or if
you're playing against each other online,
each participant can be considered a
team—whether it's just an individual or
multiple people. Each team will have to
come up with a container that can (hope-
fully) hold the egg safely when dropped
from six feet. When the teams are ready,
they must present the container to everyone and show how it works. If you're
playing against people virtually, make
sure they have their cameras positioned
so that the whole group can see the drop
zone. The team with the most sensible
container and best presentation wins.

**4 or more divided
into teams**

Eggs

Egg Head Spin-and-Attack

This is an outdoor game. Designate one part of the yard as a "safe zone." It doesn't need to be very large; just big enough for a couple of people to stand in. You will need one person to volunteer to be the spinner, and the rest will be the attackers. The spinner will hold the broom upright and steady on the ground, put his or her forehead on the top of the handle, and spin around five times. The spinner must then run across the yard and dodge the water balloons being tossed at him or her until reaching the other side of the yard. After reaching the safe zone, someone will switch places with the spinner, and the old spinner becomes an attacker. It's best to keep it up until everyone has had at least one turn being the spinner. The ones who make it without being hit by a water balloon win. Due to the use of balloons, prior to the game ensure no one is allergic to latex.

NUMBER OF PLAYERS

3 or more

WHAT YOU'LL NEED

Broom

Latex water balloons

Egg Roller Relay

Give each player an egg and have everyone go to the starting line. The object of the game is to have the players roll their egg from the starting line to the finish line and back without cracking the shell.

You can choose to have the players roll the egg using only their noses, one finger, or feet—whatever you want. The person who finishes first is, of course, the winner of the relay!

NUMBER OF PLAYERS

3 or more

WHAT YOU'LL NEED

Hard-boiled eggs, 1 for each player

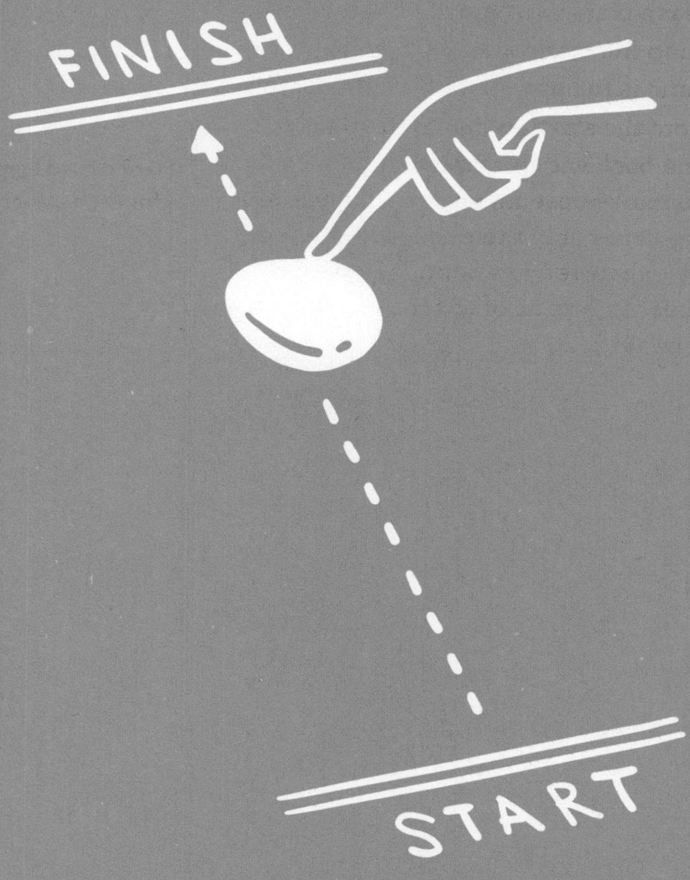
FINISH
START

Feed Me!

This is a hysterical game for the players to get a little messy. Start by having everyone break into pairs. One of the pair will put on a blindfold, and the other will put on a bib. The blindfolded person will be handed a spoon and a jar of baby food. The blindfolded players will be racing against the others to feed their partners as fast as they can without making a huge mess. You can do a second round by letting them switch positions and go again. The one with the quickest feed time and the least mess wins the game.

NUMBER OF PLAYERS

4 or more divided into pairs

WHAT YOU'LL NEED

Blindfolds

Bibs

Spoons

Assortment of jarred baby food (preferably fruit)

Fishbowl

This is a three-round game that several people can play. On each scrap of paper, write the name of a character or person whom everyone will know. Fold up each scrap and place it in the bowl. If you're playing online, one person will be designated host and in charge of creating the slips of paper.

Medium-to-large group divided into teams

Scraps of paper

Pen

Bowl

Timer

Once all the players are in a room, either in person or virtually, one person will stand up, pull a paper out of the bowl, and silently read the name without letting anyone know what it says. (If you're playing online, the host will privately message the person whose turn it is.) That person now has one minute to verbally and/or physically describe the character without saying the name. As people guess the characters correctly, the person who's giving the clues can continue pulling names and acting them out until time is up. Whoever guesses a character first gets a point, and the person giving clues gets a point for each name correctly guessed.

The first round continues until everyone has a chance to act out the characters. Once all the names are used, the second round starts. In round two, you can only act out the character. Once all the names are used in round two, round three's rule is that only one word can be used to describe the character. The same scoring applies in all three rounds.

Flip-a-Song Karaoke

Have everyone gather around the music device you have supplied, or you can have one person play the audio on his or her computer if you're gathering virtually. Ask for a volunteer to be the first singer. Allow the person to pick a song he or she knows, and set it up to play. Play the song for a moment so everyone can hear how it goes. Then cut the music off so that it is up to the singer to complete the next verse.

Here's the catch: The person must finish the song verse but use a different genre of music. For example, if the person chose a rock song, he or she could finish the verse using a country twang. If it was a slow song, he or she could turn it into a rap.

Flip-Book Frenzy

Give one person a sticky pad and pass out the black markers to everyone. Have the person with the pad draw a stick figure on the first page of the pad. Then have the person flip to the next sticky page, leaving the first page stuck to the pad, and pass the pad to the person on his or her right.

On each page, each participant should copy the drawing on the page before, only changing a small detail about the stick figure. For example, to create a kung fu flip-book story, make the figure's leg move slightly with each page until a kick has been created. Those familiar with this process can start with any art they want, as long as it works when the pages are flipped.

NUMBER OF PLAYERS

4 or more

WHAT YOU'LL NEED

Several sticky note-pads (preferably 1 for each player)

Black fine-point markers

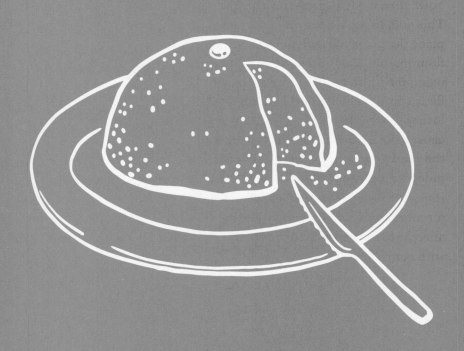

Flour Game

Pack the flour inside the bowl as tightly as you can. Place the plate on top of the bowl, turn it over, and remove the bowl. This will create a flour mound. Gently place the piece of candy on top of the flour mound. Each player then takes turns using the knife to slice off sections of flour without caving in the mound and losing the candy inside of it. The one who causes the mound to cave in must pick the candy out with the knife. This game is indeed simple, but it can become competitive, and everyone will likely want to play for more than just one round! For those allergic to gluten, substitute the flour with something else.

NUMBER OF PLAYERS

3 or more

WHAT YOU'LL NEED

Bag of flour

Medium bowl

Plate (with a circumference bigger than that of the bowl)

Piece of candy

Butter knife or plastic knife

Following the Leader

Start by gathering everyone into an area where they can hear you explain that when you ring the bell or blow the whistle, the participants must change something that they are doing.

For example, you could tell your guests that if you ring the bell, they must call out the name of the person closest to them. The person or people to do it last is/are out of the game, or can take over as host. You can change what you want them to do every time you ring the bell or blow the whistle. The last one, or last few, standing is/are the winner(s).

NUMBER OF PLAYERS

4 or more

WHAT YOU'LL NEED

Bell or whistle

Fragile-Package Toss

Have everyone pick a partner, and give
one water balloon to each pair. Have
everyone line up in a row, partners facing
each other. The object of the game is for
the partners to toss the water balloon
back and forth between them without
breaking it. Each time players catch
the balloon, they have to take a step
backward before tossing it back to their
partner. The last team with an unpopped
water balloon wins the game! Due to the
use of balloons, before the game make
sure no one is allergic to latex.

NUMBER OF PLAYERS

4 or more divided
into teams of 2

WHAT YOU'LL NEED

One prefilled latex
water balloon for
each team

Freeze

At the beginning of the dinner or any get-together, designate someone as Mr. or Ms. Freeze. At some point in the evening, that person will freeze, and everyone else must also freeze. The last person to do so becomes the new Mr. or Ms. Freeze. The winner of the game is the person who doesn't freeze at all.

NUMBER OF PLAYERS

4 or more

WHAT YOU'LL NEED

N/A

Going on a Picnic

Players in person or online can pretend they are going on a picnic. They begin by saying, "I'm going on a picnic and I'm bringing..." People have to say what the person/persons before them said plus what they are bringing. If they skip an item or can't remember, they are out. The last person to recite the list correctly wins. An alternate way to play is to use the alphabet. Each turn will require that item to begin with the next letter in the alphabet.

NUMBER OF PLAYERS

4 or more

WHAT YOU'LL NEED

N/A

Grand Tour

This game is somewhat like the game known as Telephone. As the first guest arrives, either to your home or to the video conference room, give that person a tour of your home (or the video conference room). As you go through the rooms, name something that you plan to do with the room, or to decorate it with. As the next guest arrives, the first guest will then give that person the tour, repeating each thing you said. The next guest will be given the tour by the previous guest, following the same rules. If you're playing online, the virtual host will walk everyone through their home, showing off the rooms through the camera as the guests narrate.

Once the last tour has taken place, the final guest will take everyone on a tour, repeating what he or she was told. As you can imagine, hilarious things tend to come out as the guests struggle to remember what was actually said.

NUMBER OF PLAYERS

6 or more

WHAT YOU'LL NEED

N/A

Guess That Tune

This game is going to test how familiar everyone is with past and current music. The catch is that the players themselves have to hum the tune. Before you begin playing, write down on each scrap of paper popular songs from the past and ones that are currently popular. Place the scraps in the container or bowl and mix them up. Have everyone pull a paper and hum the tune until someone can guess what it is. For every tune they guess correctly, players receive one point. The player with the most points at the end wins the game.

NUMBER OF PLAYERS

4 or more

WHAT YOU'LL NEED

Scraps of paper

Pen

Container or bowl

Gum Bobbing

It's best to prepare this one when none of the players are in the room—that way they don't know where on the plate you have placed the gum. Put a piece of unwrapped gum on each plate and cover the gum and plate in whipped cream. The object of the game is for players to retrieve the gum without using their hands, chew it, and blow a bubble before anyone else does. The first one to blow the bubble wins the game.

3 or more

Bubble gum

Paper plates

Whipped cream

Head Pendulum

First line up the bottles, spreading them out in a circle. Have one person stand in the middle. He or she will need to put the baseball in the bottom of one leg of the pantyhose. He or she will then need to slide the waist of the pantyhose over his or her head and tie it tight with the empty leg of the hose.

Once the pantyhose are secure, the player will place his or her hands behind the back and try to knock down all of the bottles without using hands or feet, swinging the ball in the hose like a pendulum. If the player knocks them down in a minute or less, he or she wins the challenge.

WHAT YOU'LL NEED

6 empty plastic water bottles

Baseball

Pair of pantyhose

Stopwatch

Hide-and-Seek

This is the old children's game but with a twist that makes it a fun game for adults and kids alike. One person is chosen to be "it." She or he has ten minutes to find a hiding place, and then the others start searching for the person. But—and this is where the twist comes—when one of the other players finds the person hiding, she or he hides with that person. The searcher doesn't have to do this right away; she or he can wait for the other players to leave the area. This continues, with more and more of the players hiding together instead of seeking until there's only one searcher left. If you want the game to move fast, set a time for the searching; anyone who hasn't found the person/people in hiding at the end of the allotted time is knocked out for the next round.

4 or more

A large house or property

Homemade Ball Toss

Lay the tarp out flat and cut four holes big enough for a football to go through. Paint around the outside of the cutouts and mark one with five points, one with ten points, one with fifteen points, and one with twenty points. While this is drying, cut four lengths of nylon rope to hang the tarp with. If there aren't any grommets already on the tarp, you can cut a hole in each corner and run the rope through.

Once everything is dry, hang the tarp and let the participants take turns trying to throw the ball through the holes for points. The player with the most points at the end wins the game.

NUMBER OF PLAYERS

3 or more

WHAT YOU'LL NEED

A medium-sized tarp

Scissors

Paint

Nylon rope

Ball

Hoop Toss

This outdoor game is a larger version of Ring Toss. Place the barstools or chairs randomly around the yard. Have the first player stand about ten feet from the first stool and try to toss a Hula-Hoop over the stool. Leave it wherever it lands and give that person the next hoop. That person will try to make it over the next stool and do the same with the last Hula-Hoop and stool. Once that person's turn has ended, gather the Hula-Hoops up and bring them back to where the players are standing so that others can try. The following players will step up, one by one, and toss the three hoops. The player to get the most Hula-Hoops around the stools—or closest to the stools—wins the game.

NUMBER OF PLAYERS

3 or more

WHAT YOU'LL NEED

3 barstools or chairs

3 Hula-Hoops

Horse

Shooting baskets has never been so fun than with a game of Horse. In this game, the players will take turns shooting the ball, trying to make a basket. The first player who makes a basket gets an "H." Every time that person makes a basket after that, another letter is gained until *horse* is spelled.

The catch is that wherever the basket is made from or however it is made originally, the following players must do the same to get their letter. If no one has made a basket for a full round, then people can choose where they want to stand and how they will shoot their ball to try to make it harder for everyone else to compete. The first to spell *horse* wins the game.

NUMBER OF PLAYERS

3 or more

WHAT YOU'LL NEED

Basketball

Basketball hoop or large empty trash can

Household Scavenger Hunt

Make a list of things that can be found around the house. These can be found all over the house, or even in the yard. Try to come up with some tricky things to find. You can also be creative with your descriptions. Copy the list and give it to each of the players. Time the hunt; first one back at the starting point who's found everything on the list is the winner.

NUMBER OF PLAYERS

2 or more

WHAT YOU'LL NEED

Notebooks

Pens

How's Yours?

Guessing games are always fun, and this guessing game is great to play in person or together virtually. Have everyone gather in a group and select one player to be the "odd person out." This player will step out of the room or away from hearing distance of the group. Pick an item everybody has in common, like a car. When the odd person out is asked back, each player is to say one word—and *only* one word—that applies to the chosen item. For a car, people could say the color, the place it comes from, that it's fast or that it's dirty, or anything to describe it in one word. The odd person out has to try to guess what it is they are talking about, and this usually prompts hilarious answers. The players can create a "red herring" to misdirect the odd person out; for example, they might try to make the person think they're talking about an office chair, which has wheels. Make sure the words aren't too direct. When the player has guessed the selected item or has given up, a new odd person out can be chosen.

4 or more

N/A

Hungry Puzzler

First, cut the magazine page into sections and give everyone a piece of the picture. (Do not tell anyone what the larger picture shows.) Next, give everyone some cereal, glue, and a card and tell them to use the cereal to try to re-create the portion of the image they were given (gluing the cereal to the card). Once everyone is done, gather all the cards together and try to figure out what the original picture was. You can split people into groups and see who figures out the puzzle first. Whoever gets it right first is the winner!

4 or more

Magazine page with a picture of people engaged in an activity (for example, playing sports or cooking)

Scissors

Assortment of cereal

Glue

4" × 6" cards

Hurry! Hurry! Make the List

Before you play, you'll need to create about fifteen or so lists of finite categories (for example, women who've won the Best Actress Oscar, Super Bowl participants from the past ten years, etc.). Have someone blindly choose one of the lists. Each participant has five seconds to name someone or something on the list. Whoever can't drops out. The last person in the game gets a point for that list. Whoever has the most points at the end of the evening wins.

4 or more

Lists

Improv in a Bag

It's time to brush up on your creativity and improvisation skills! This game challenges players to use their acting skills, as well as teamwork. Divide players into pairs or teams and give each team a bag of random household items as props to create a skit. Each team has ten minutes to come up with a skit by using every item in the bag. The catch is that the players cannot use the items for what their actual purpose is.

For example, if someone is given a spoon, that person can't use it to insinuate eating but could use it as a drumstick to pretend playing the drums. Once time is up, the players from each team must perform their skit in front of the rest of the group. Performing is fun in and of itself, but you can also make this a point-based game by giving each household item a point value depending on the difficulty in using it, and the team who has the most points at the end wins. If there is a tie in the end, then the teams will have to perform one last skit, and the other teams will vote on whose was the best.

4 or more divided into teams

A bag for each team

Random items from around the house

Ingredients Throw-Down

For this, you will have everyone helping to prepare dinner and dessert. Once everyone is ready, you will need to assign everyone a course: appetizer, main dish, or dessert. If there are more than three people participating, you can assign multiple people to one course. Give each course a limited amount of ingredients and tell everyone they now have a time limit (thirty minutes for appetizer, one hour for dinner, and one hour for dessert) to create a dish for their category.

They can use any cooking staple they like, such as butter, oil, dressings, and spices. But they have to include each main ingredient you have given them. Once time is up, everyone gets to try the appetizer and judge the dish. Next, everyone will enjoy dinner, soon followed by dessert. The most creative and best tasting dish wins the challenge.

NUMBER OF PLAYERS

3 or more

WHAT YOU'LL NEED

Variety of food ingredients

Timer

Cooking utensils

Job Charades

Have everyone grab index cards and write down some jobs and careers. Suggest they think out of the box; that way, there will be fewer repeats with the cards. Have them drop the cards in a bowl, and one by one, have the guests come up and pull a card. They are now left with the task of acting out the career or job on the card. If you want to enjoy this game with a group online, have participants submit their suggestions to the host, and the host can privately message the person acting out the jobs. You can do a point system where the person with the most correct guesses wins, or just have fun with it.

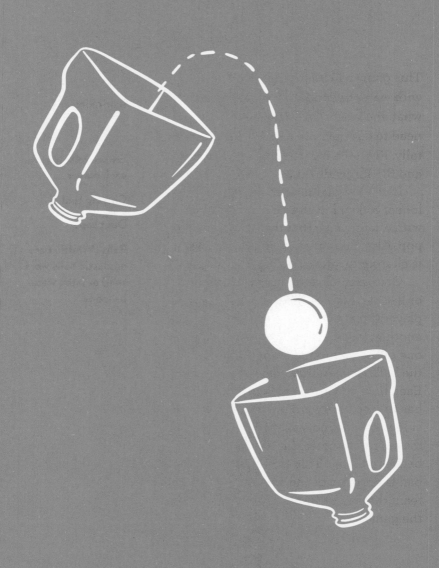

Jug Master

This game can be played with balls or with water balloons. It just depends on what you prefer for that day. You will need to cut the milk jugs in half horizontally. Keep the half that has the handle and flip it upside down.

If you are planning to use water balloons, you will need to cover the edges with duct tape so that the balloons won't pop. Also, beforehand, make sure no one is allergic to latex.

Give each player a jug and have him or her partner up with someone. Have the players start by standing across from one another, face-to-face. Place one ball in one of the teams' jugs. They will then toss the ball between them using their jugs. Each time someone catches it, he or she has to step backward one step and to the side (one side moves left, while the other moves right, increasing the distance between them). This continues until the ball is dropped or the balloon breaks. The team that is farthest apart at the end wins the game.

4 or more

Empty milk jugs for each player

Cutting tool

Duct tape

Balls (Whiffle balls or plastic balls work well) or latex water balloons

Leap Spoon

For this game, you will need to line up three glasses in a row. Lay the spoons on the table. When the timer starts, players will begin flipping the spoons, in a single motion, by hitting the round ends. The object of the game is for players to flip a spoon into each glass. The spoons must touch the bottom of the inside of the glasses for them to count. If someone can complete this before time is up, he or she wins.

NUMBER OF PLAYERS

3 or more

WHAT YOU'LL NEED

3 glasses

6 spoons

Timer

Mad Lib Story

Have the players gather around the board or paper, or, if you're playing virtually, gather in a video conference room. The leader asks the group to name ten random items, followed by ten random locations and ten random people. Write it all down on the board, or, if you're playing online, have the leader type all the words into a document and share their screen.

Once the list is complete, the leader asks for a volunteer to start, revealing that it is a storytelling game. The player must choose one word from the list and make up five sentences in a story that each has the word incorporated into it. Then the next person chooses a word and continues the story with five new sentences. The last person must wrap up the story.

NUMBER OF PLAYERS

4 or more

WHAT YOU'LL NEED

Large board or paper to write on

Masquerade

Making a mask is a great way to express one's self. You can be anything behind that mask—a superhero, a bird, or even an alien. It becomes whatever your mind thinks up. Supply the participants with pastels and have them color their masks to their liking. Once they are done, you will need to spray a coat of fixative spray over the masks to make sure the colors stay on and do not bleed. For a further challenge, you can get an assortment of sequins, feathers, and other decorative items to glue on the masks. Once they are dry, let everyone roam around wearing the masks and pretending to be whatever they like. Then vote on which mask is the most creative.

NUMBER OF PLAYERS

4 or more

WHAT YOU'LL NEED

Pastels

Plain white papier-mâché masks

Pastel fixative spray

Minute-to-Win-It Iron Man

Give each player a set of chopsticks and put the nuts where the players can reach them easily. Using the chopsticks, the players have three minutes to stack as many of the nuts in a tower in front of them as they can. If their tower falls down before the three minutes are up, they can start again. The person who builds the tallest tower wins the game.

2 or more

As many sets of chopsticks as there are players

A bunch of small iron nuts

Stopwatch

Model Drawing

Ever dreamed about being a model or perhaps the muse for someone else's creations? This game gives everyone a shot at modeling, whether that's in person or in a virtual hangout. Have everyone take turns being the model for others to try to draw. They can do serious poses or funny poses—it's up to them. Once they are done with their drawings, vote on which one is the most insightful and creative.

NUMBER OF PLAYERS

1 or more

WHAT YOU'LL NEED

Paper

Drawing utensils

Monkey See, Monkey Do

This is a variation on Charades. Select a person and whisper something that you want that person to act out to the rest of the group. This person cannot speak, only move around. When someone guesses correctly, the person who has been acting gets to tell that person what to act out. This continues until everyone has had a turn.

NUMBER OF PLAYERS

4 or more

WHAT YOU'LL NEED

N/A

Most Likely To...

Players sit in a circle facing one another, or gather in a video conference room. One person says the phrase "Most likely to..." and ends it with some characteristic (for instance, "Get a job," "Earn a million dollars in one year," or "Write a book"). Everyone then says the name of someone she or he thinks that phrase describes. The person with the most votes is out. The game continues until only one person is left; that person is the winner.

4 or more

Enough chairs that all players can sit in a circle

Movie and Show Trivia

This game works best if you use an assortment of TV shows and movies from all eras and types. You will need to prepare half of the index cards to be TV shows, keeping them on one color card, and the other half to be movies, printed or written on the other color card. Write down a description of the show/movie on the front of the card, and below the description give four lettered options for show/movie titles. At the very bottom of the card, in small print, write which letter is the correct choice.

When everyone is ready, have them sit in front of you. Go around and ask the players if they want to do show or movie trivia. Once they have chosen, pull that card, read it, and see if they can get the right answer. For every incorrect answer, you will tuck the card back into the stack without revealing the correct answer. If someone gets it correct, hand that person the card. It's a good way to keep count of how many correct responses each person has had. The player with the most cards at the end of the game is the trivia winner.

Movie Trivia

Have everyone write down two to three popular movie titles on the pieces of paper. Fold them up and place the papers in a bowl or container. After mixing them up, have everyone take turns pulling a title and then acting it out. The first to successfully guess the correct movie title gets to go next. If no one can guess the title, then the player has to go again. You can break into teams if you'd like and, when acting out, can even use a timer set at two minutes. The team that the actor is on has to guess within the time limit to earn a point. The team with the most points at the end wins.

Mug Shots

Uh-oh, everyone's been busted! They are in trouble and have to have their mug shot taken. Create a mug shot card using the camera, the board, and the markers. Go one-by-one and put their name on the board and the reason they were arrested. If you're gathering together online, share your screen with an image of the mug shot. This could be anything you can think of, but funny is always best. Once you are done, send the photos to your guests or, if they're okay with it, post them online.

NUMBER OF PLAYERS

5 or more

WHAT YOU'LL NEED

Camera

Small dry-erase board

Dry-erase markers

Mummy Wrap

For this game you will need players to split into pairs or teams. Give each team a roll of toilet paper. They must wrap up one of their teammates like a mummy, using the entire roll of toilet paper. The first team to wrap its mummy from head to toe is the winner of the game.

NUMBER OF PLAYERS

4 or more (divisible by 2)

WHAT YOU'LL NEED

2 rolls of toilet paper

Murder Mystery Game

When you invite everyone to play, make sure to note that it is a murder mystery party. It's always best to set a theme for a murder mystery. Some popular themes are casino, train, 1920s, 1950s, Mardi Gras, Halloween, and Western. Having everyone dress the part will help to create a more engaging atmosphere, but it isn't necessary. You will need to create basic character descriptions for each person attending, whether that's in person or virtually, supplying each character's career and role in the mystery, along with a clue. Here are some examples.

NUMBER OF PLAYERS

6 or more

WHAT YOU'LL NEED

Pen

Paper

Props appropriate for chosen theme

- **Waiter:** You waited on the table of the victim the night of the murder.
  - **Clue:** The victim complained about your service and didn't leave a tip.
- **Musician:** You played piano at the dueling piano bar that the victim frequented every weekend.
  - **Clue:** The victim always tipped big and flaunted money in the bar.
- **Struggling Comedian:** You were the performing act at the location that the victim was murdered.
  - **Clue:** The victim was heckling you shortly before the murder.

- **Lawyer:** You were the lawyer for the victim and his multimillion-dollar company.
  - **Clue:** You were aware of all of the victim's offshore accounts and had access to them.

You will also need filler characters like these: bartender, dancer, elderly couple, private investigator, singer, cousin, etc. Just make sure to create enough to assign everyone a character identity, and these characters should also have a clue that somehow links them to the murderer. That way, when everyone is being questioned, the clues are there to help point out the real murderer.

To begin this Murder Mystery Game, you will need to gather your guests into one room, whether that's in person or virtually, and announce that there has been a murder. You will now say where, when, and how the victim was murdered. Everyone then tries to figure out who the murderer is. Everyone in the room is now a suspect.

Have all the guests close their eyes, and you will circle the room and tap the preplanned murderer on the shoulder. If you're playing online, the host can private message the murderer. Have guests open their eyes, and inform them that the person who was tapped is the murderer, and it must remain a secret. People will begin their investigations by questioning each other based on the available clues. The murderer is free to implicate anyone in the room he or she likes, to try to throw the scent off him or her and confuse the others. Once everyone has been questioned, and all clues have been gathered, the guests can reveal whom they believe the murderer is. The first person to guess correctly wins the Murder Mystery Game.

Musical Balance

This is just like Musical Chairs, but with an awesome twist. Prepare some music to play in the background during the game. Hand the players a book each and tell them they will need to balance it on their head. When the music starts, they will walk around the room, keeping the book balanced. When the music stops, all the players must stop and kneel down on one knee. If their book drops, they are out. Once the music starts again, the remaining players have to stand back up and continue to walk around the room until the music stops again. The last person with the book still balanced on his or her head wins the game.

4 or more

Background music

A book for each player

Musical Teacups

Place around the table all but one teacup for each person playing. Have the players gather around the table as well. When the music begins, everyone will circle the table. When the music stops, everyone must grab a teacup. The person without a teacup is out of the game. Take away one teacup. The game continues until there is only one person left.

NUMBER OF PLAYERS

4 or more

WHAT YOU'LL NEED

Teacups

Table with chairs

Music

Name the Celebrity

This trivia game requires a little bit of research to prepare. You will need to choose at least twenty celebrities of all ages and types of acting or music. Cut out a photo of a celebrity, glue it to the poster board, and write in marker a number below the photo. Next write down, for your eyes only, several movies each thespian was in. For musicians, write down lyrics from songs they have performed.

When everyone is ready, have them take a seat in front of the celebrity poster board. Hand each player a pen and paper. You will begin by naming two films that a celebrity on the board was in or lyrics they sang, without saying the name. The players must write down the name of the celebrity they think it is and the number they have on the board. Once you have gone through each celebrity, collect the papers. The player with the most correct trivia answers wins the game.

4 or more

Old magazines

Scissors

Glue

Poster board

Marker

Pens

Paper

Name the Difference

Start by having two people enter the room. Everyone playing the game must observe them. They then leave the room and either switch, remove, or alter one thing about themselves. When they return to the room, the players must name what the differences for each one are. The player with the most accurate observation wins. You can also play this game with friends and family online. Rather than have people leave the room, you can have them get out of the view of their cameras.

4 or more

N/A

Never Have I Ever

Hand everyone three pennies to use as scorekeepers. The first person starts by saying, "Never have I ever..." and then says something he or she has never done before. For example, players could say, "Never have I ever been on an airplane," "Never have I ever swam in a public pool," "Never have I ever lied to my parents," and "Never have I ever eaten broccoli." All of the players who have done that named thing forfeit a penny.

When the next person goes, he or she will offer another example. If someone runs out of pennies, he or she must then do a dare in order to gain three pennies back. The player or players with the most pennies win(s) the game. To avoid this game becoming inappropriate, just set the ground rule that all comments need to be clean and suitable for all ears.

NUMBER OF PLAYERS

2 or more

WHAT YOU'LL NEED

Pennies (about 10 per person)

HELLO
my name is
LOOPY
Leonard

HELLO
my name is
Excited
Erica

HELLO
my name is
TOUGH
TOM

Nickname Name Tag

This little game is sure to get participants laughing at themselves and others. As everyone enters the room, give him or her a name tag and a marker. Everyone should approach someone who is not already assigned a nickname and then give that person a nickname, using the first letter of the person's name to choose the nickname. For example, nicknames could include Tough Tom, Loopy Leonard, Smart Sharon, or Excited Erica. The person given the name can come up with a nickname for that person, or find another person to name. (Each person nicknames only one other person, though.) Once everyone has a filled-in name tag, have them take a turn explaining whether their new nickname suits them or is far from the truth.

NUMBER OF PLAYERS

4 or more

WHAT YOU'LL NEED

Name tags

Markers

Noodling Around

Start this one by placing the penne pasta on the table. At the start of the game, the players must stand with their hands beside them. On "Go," the players will grab a piece of spaghetti and put one end in their mouth. They now have to pick up six pieces of the penne pasta with the spaghetti noodle. The penne cannot enter their mouth, and if the spaghetti noodle breaks, they can continue to play only if it is still long enough to gather all six pieces. If it is too small, they are disqualified. If a penne drops off the noodle, it can still be used if it lands on the table. If it bounces off, the player is disqualified. Whoever is first to gather the six pieces wins the game.

2 or more

Dry penne pasta

Dry spaghetti noodles

Office Chair Catapult

This game is a great way to use up some free time at work, utilize your home office, or just turn any chair into a fun game. Take a chair and flip it upside down. Run a rubber band around two of the legs to act as a slingshot, and use wadded-up paper for your launching items. The object of the game is to get one of the paper wads to land on a desk or table and stay there. Score a point for each wad that lands. Decide how many rounds you want to play and then tally the points to decide the winner.

NUMBER OF PLAYERS

2 or more

WHAT YOU'LL NEED

Chair with 4 legs

Large rubber bands

Wadded-up paper

Office desk

Office Supply Fishing

Begin this game by tying a string to the end of a pencil. At the end of the string, attach a paper clip that has been unfolded and pinched into the shape of a hook. Place a set of keys on the floor. Players now have to fish the keys up from the floor using the office fishing rod. Each person then passes the rod to someone else. The person who succeeds in fishing the keys in the shortest time wins the game.

NUMBER OF PLAYERS

2 or more

WHAT YOU'LL NEED

String

Pencil

Paper clip

Keys

Stopwatch

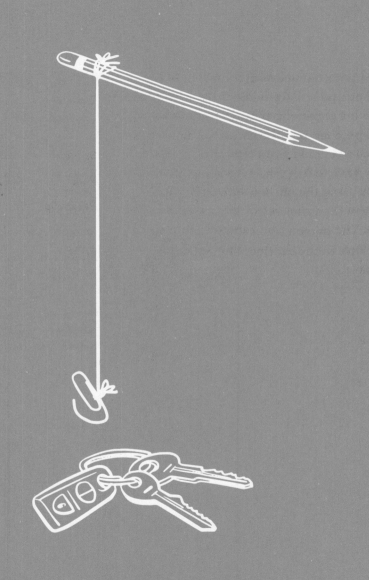

On Your Mark, Get Set, Draw!

One person from each team stands next to one of the pads of paper with a marker. The other team member chooses a strip from the bowl and shows it (without looking at it) to the player standing by his or her pad. Those people have one minute to draw the object named on the paper strip. While they are doing this, the other member of their team tries to guess what the object is. The first one to guess right gets a point. At the end, the team with the most points wins.

NUMBER OF PLAYERS

4 or more divided into teams of 2

WHAT YOU'LL NEED

Several large pads of paper

Easels or something on which to display the pads

Markers

Strips of paper with names of objects written on them, mixed in a bowl

Stopwatch

Ostrich Dance

This is played by two people at a time. One of those not playing in the round selects two cards and tapes one to each player's back. The object is to read the word on your opponent's back. The player who does so first wins the round. Then two more players play. When all players have gone, the winning players play one another until only one is left. That person is the winner.

NUMBER OF PLAYERS

4 or more

WHAT YOU'LL NEED

Index cards with random words written on them (*not* to be shown to the players)

Tape

Our Future and Then...

Have everyone take a pen and paper
and have a seat. Select one couple. The
object of the game is to start with the
phrase "And then...." People are to write
down two to three sentences describing
what the couple will do. They can get as
silly as they like with their descriptions.
Once everyone is done, you will gather
the papers and mix them up. Start telling
the story of their future like this: "After
[insert couple's name] decided to live
together, they drove away together, and
then..." Next read one of the papers, followed by the next, and continue until you
have run out of papers. Then go on to
another couple until you've gone through
everyone. And if you want to have a virtual couples' night, you can play with
each couple videoing from their own
couch and reading their own "And then..."
entries. You can decide whose story was
the funniest/craziest, and that couple is
the winner.

2 couples or more

Paper

Pens

Paper Scraper

With this game, the players will use index cards to build a ten-story "paper scraper." Fold all but ten of the index cards in half. When the game starts, players will begin by placing two of the bent cards on the table side by side. Players top these with a flat index card and then two more of the bent cards. The first person to get ten stories high and have his or her paper scraper stay intact for at least three seconds wins the game.

NUMBER OF PLAYERS

3 or more

WHAT YOU'LL NEED

30 index cards

Stopwatch

Pass the Mango

Have your guests divide into two teams. The players, each standing six feet from their nearest teammate, will tuck a mango under their chin and shoulder, race over to their teammates, and pass the mango to them without using their hands. The person it's being passed to cannot use his or her hands to receive it. If the mango is dropped, it can be picked up and put back in between the player's shoulder and chin, but then the team must start back over with the first person. The first team to pass the mango to every team member and cross the finish line without dropping it wins.

NUMBER OF PLAYERS

4 or more divided into 2 teams

WHAT YOU'LL NEED

Mangoes (1 per team)

Pin the Mullet on the Dude

This is a spin on a classic game most everyone is familiar with: Pin the Tail on the Donkey. Since mullets were all the rage in the eighties, this is the perfect game for an eighties-themed party. Have everyone line up to take a shot at pinning the mullet on the dude. Each player will take turns putting on the blindfold and trying to pin the mullet on the best he or she can. The player with the closest pin wins the game.

4 or more

Large picture of a bald guy dressed like he's from the 1980s

Cutout of a mullet

Double-sided tape

Blindfold

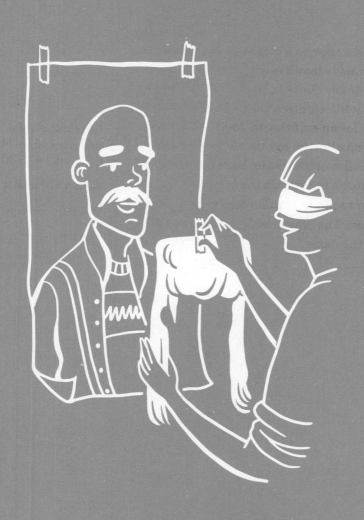

Plastic Wrap

Wrap the object in plastic wrap. Continue wrapping it until you've used the entire package of plastic wrap. Set the timer for one minute and hand the ball of plastic wrap to the first player. She or he has one minute to unwrap as much of the ball as possible. After one minute has passed, hand the ball to the next player. The player who succeeds in unwrapping the object completely wins the game.

NUMBER OF PLAYERS

2 or more

WHAT YOU'LL NEED

A package of plastic wrap

A small object such as a piece of candy, trinket, etc.

Timer

Prediction Bingo

This works best at a gathering where
most people are familiar with one
another. When everyone gathers either
in person or online, hand them a blank
bingo card and marker or pen, or have
them create their own if you're video
conferencing. They must fill in the blank
spaces on the card with their predictions
for the party. For example, people can
write what they think a particular person
will say, who will be late, or whatever they
believe will happen during the evening.
After everyone has filled in a bingo card,
they will mark the things off as they happen during the get-together. The person
with the most correct predictions on his
or her card at the end of the game wins.

NUMBER OF PLAYERS

6 or more

WHAT YOU'LL NEED

Blank bingo cards
(printed out from the
Internet, or you can
make them yourself)

Markers or pens

Presentation Memory

A game like this will help everyone learn a little about one another. Have players gather at least three to four items that mean something to them. Have the players get in a circle or sign into a video conference room if playing virtually and place their items in front of them. The first player holds up one item and says something about it, perhaps a memory or its special meaning. He or she is to do this for each item and, once completed, place the items out of everyone's sight. The next person is to do the same.

When everyone has finished talking about their items, the players have to take turns holding up an item and having the other players buzz in to correctly recite what the memory or special meaning was. The person with the most correct items wins the game. It can get complicated when people get very detailed about their items.

4 or more

Personal items of each player

Psychologist

The people playing this game must know one another pretty well. One person is chosen as the "psychologist" and sent out of the room, or signs out of the virtual hangout. The others agree to switch personalities; for instance, everyone takes on the personality of the person sitting to his or her left. Online players can choose a player's personality ahead of time. Once this has been agreed upon, the "psychologist" comes back into the room or signs back into the video conference and is told, "Doctor, we have a problem, and we need you to figure out what it is. You can ask us questions about anything in our lives." As the "doctor" starts asking questions, each player answers the way they think the person sitting to their left would. The game continues until the "psychologist" figures it out.

NUMBER OF PLAYERS

4 or more

WHAT YOU'LL NEED

N/A

Puff Ball Fight

It doesn't have to be cold or snowing outside to have a snowball fight, but you will probably want to play this one outside to avoid things getting too messy. With these snowless puff balls, you can start the fight any time of the year. To prepare the puff balls, you will need to fill the foot part of the pantyhose with about a half cup of flour, cut an inch above the flour, pull tight, and tie off.

Continue filling the pantyhose up, making sure to tie off one end before putting in the flour, and follow up with tying it off to contain the flour. You should get around five puff balls per leg. Since these puff balls do not bust right away, giving everyone two or three each works just fine.

You can choose to set up teams or to play the game as individual players. However you opt to play, design your scoreboard after that. Each time a player makes contact with another player using the puff balls, he or she will receive a point. The player or team with the most points at the end wins.

4 or more

Pantyhose

Flour

Measuring cup

Paper and pen for keeping score

Room Recall

Take everyone to a room of your choice. Open the door, let them view the room for one minute, and let them know that they must try to remember as much about the room as possible. Then close the door. Hand them each a piece of paper and some crayons, and have them re-create the room from memory.

This game is a little funnier if you have some truly random items lying around the room, like a stuffed cat, a bowl of socks, or anything that might strike someone as odd. The person who draws the room the most accurately wins the game. You can give bonus points for the odd items in the room if they are featured in their art.

NUMBER OF PLAYERS

4 or more

WHAT YOU'LL NEED

Paper

Crayons

Rorschach Test

Choose one person to be the referee and one person to hold up one of the ink blots so everyone can see it. Each of the players (including the one holding the blot) writes down what she or he thinks it looks like, trying to be as imaginative as possible. The players put their names on their descriptions of the blot and pass them secretly to the referee, or privately message the referee if playing together virtually. The referee reads each description aloud, and the players try to guess who wrote it. The player at the end who made the most right guesses wins.

NUMBER OF PLAYERS

4 or more

WHAT YOU'LL NEED

5–6 Rorschach ink blots (make these by dripping some ink on a piece of paper, folding it in half, unfolding it, and letting it dry)

Paper

Pencils

Shakedown

Several people can play this at once. Tape a string securely around the tissue box. Fill the box with bouncy balls, and one at a time have the players tie the box around their waist like a belt with the opening in the box pointing down. Set the stopwatch for one minute. When the minute starts, players will need to shake as much as possible to get all of the balls to fall out of the tissue box. Whoever is successful wins the game.

NUMBER OF PLAYERS

4 or more

WHAT YOU'LL NEED

Tape

String

Empty tissue box

Bag of bouncy balls

Stopwatch

Shoes Up

This game demonstrates how couples see their relationship. Place two chairs back-to-back and have one half of the couple sit in one chair and the other half sit in the other. Have them take their shoes off and hand one shoe to the other person. They will need to hold one of their shoes in one hand and their partner's shoe in the other hand. You will then ask them a series of questions, and they will hold up the shoe of the person the question pertains to.

For example, you could ask, "Who does the dishes most between the two of you?" They will then hold up the shoe of who they believe does the dishes the most. Have someone keep score on how many times they agree during the questioning.

Slippery Dash

This is an outdoor game. Lay out your plastic sheeting and put a yard stake in each corner to keep it posted to the ground. Make the sheeting nice and slippery using the dish soap and hose. Once it is ready to go, place two empty buckets at one end and two water-filled buckets at the other end. Have the players split up into two teams and tell them to line up next to the bucket with the water in it. Hand a plastic cup to the first player in each line. When the game begins, the players must fill their cup and race across the slippery tarp to the other side. When they get to the other side, they need to dump the water into the empty bucket. They will then rush back to the other side and hand the cup to the next player on their team. Depending on how many players you have, you can play until everyone has had two turns, or you can play until one team has filled their bucket up.

NUMBER OF PLAYERS

4 or more divided into 2 teams

WHAT YOU'LL NEED

Plastic sheeting (a tarp would work as well)

Yard stakes

Dish soap

Hose

4 buckets

2 plastic cups

Sneak a Peek

Build a structure from the blocks and place it somewhere no one can see it. Split the players into teams and give each team a set of blocks. One person from each group will go over to where the structure is and observe it for fifteen seconds and then return to his or her group. The observer must describe it so that his or her team can build a replica with their blocks.

After two minutes of building, another team member from each group will go over and observe the structure for fifteen seconds. Then that person will return to his or her group and try to fix any mistakes to make it look the same as the original structure. This will continue until the groups have made a complete replica of the structure. The first team to complete it wins.

NUMBER OF PLAYERS

6 or more

WHAT YOU'LL NEED

Children's building blocks

Song Charades

All you really need for this game is knowledge of songs. On each scrap of paper, write down the name of a song and place the scraps in a bowl. Have everyone gather around and pick a person to start the game. The person will pull the name of a song out of the bowl and act out the name without saying anything. The person who guesses correctly wins that round and gets to pull the next song and act it out. The person who guesses the most correct titles wins the game.

NUMBER OF PLAYERS

2 or more

WHAT YOU'LL NEED

Scraps of paper

Pen

Bowl

Soul Mate

Before everyone gets together, whether in person or online, you will need to write down a list of at least seven questions for the couples to answer. You can ask things like "Where did we first meet?"; "What is my favorite hobby?"; "Who was my first kiss?"; and anything that pertains to them and their relationship. When the game begins, you will need to separate the partners and put them in different rooms. Go to one room, hand each person a pen and paper, and ask him or her the questions. The players must write down their answers on the paper. Or, if you're playing virtually, private message the partners separately through the video platform or have them send answers via text or email.

Once you are done, you will have the couples reunite in the same room. You will ask the question of the one partner, and after the response, you will read the answer the partner gave. For each correctly answered question, the couple receives a point. The couple with the most points at the end of the game wins.

3 or more couples

Paper

Pen

Spice Savvy

Before you assemble the players, prepare a few plates with peppers in one area, spicy sauces in another, and some spicy appetizers in a third area. Everyone will have to challenge one another to a spice match.

For example, someone will pick a person and say, "I bet you couldn't handle a bite of a jalapeño." This person can refuse or accept the challenge. If she or he refuses, that person doesn't proceed to the next stage of the game. If the player accepts, both of them have to take a bite, chew, and swallow without taking a drink or eating a piece of bread for at least a minute after ingestion. If both make it, they move on to another challenge. If either one drinks any liquids before the minute is up, he or she loses. The trash can is there in case someone needs to spit out the spicy item. Also make sure to have plenty of milk on hand, as well as bread, to help alleviate the effects of the spices, and make sure no one has any food allergies. It's best to be safe. The person who ingests the spiciest item or lasts the longest wins the game.

NUMBER OF PLAYERS

4 or more

WHAT YOU'LL NEED

Assortment of spicy foods, peppers, and sauces

Water

Bread

Trash can

Milk

Spoon Brainteaser

You and one other person will need to know how this brainteaser works to pull it off successfully. One person is the "spoon photographer" and the other person is the "mind reader." The mind reader steps into another room. The photographer will use the spoon to "take a picture" of one of the guests' faces. Once the picture is taken, the mind reader will be called back into the room and handed the spoon. He or she will look at the spoon and stare for a moment and then reveal whose photo was taken. Continue to do this until everyone gives up or figures it out. You can even let others take a shot at being the mind reader.

The trick to this brainteaser is that the photographer has to sit in the exact same position as the person whose photo was taken. That way the mind reader can come in and, at a glance, know who the person is. If by chance the person is sitting in the same position as someone else, the mind reader will have to wait to guess until the person repositions or moves a little. This will certainly pique everyone else's interest.

Silver spoon

Spoons

Place the spoons in the middle of the table where they're easily reachable by all the players. Each player is dealt four cards. The dealer takes the top card from the deck and passes it or one of the cards from his or her hand to the player on the left. All the other players in turn pass one card from their hand to the left (note that play is continuous; the dealer takes another card and passes one *as soon as* he or she has passed the last one to the left). The last player before the dealer discards to a trash pile.

All the players are trying to make four of a kind. When a player succeeds in that, he or she takes a spoon from the pile on the middle of the table. The player can be sneaky about this and try to avoid being noticed. That's important because as soon as someone notices a spoon is missing, that person can grab one as well. The person left without a spoon loses the round and gets a letter in the word *spoon*. Spell *spoon* and you're out of the game!

NUMBER OF PLAYERS

4 or more

WHAT YOU'LL NEED

Spoons, 1 fewer than the number of people playing

Standard deck of 52 playing cards

Stack Me

The objective of this game is to return the cups, turned upside down, into a nested stack. When the clock starts, the player will take the upside-down cups and stack them (still upside down) one by one, placing an index card in between each layer, using both hands to stack the cups. Once they are set up, the player must remove the index cards, starting with the top one, using one hand only. The player is done once all the cups are nested back in a stack. The player wins this challenge only if he or she can get it all done before one minute is up and not dropping any of the cups. If players don't complete the task, they're out of the game; everyone keeps going until only one person is left.

4 or more

Stopwatch

5 plastic cups

4 index cards

Steal the Bacon

This is a great team game to play outside. Split the participants into two evenly sized teams. Each team stands in a line so the teams are facing each other, at least fifteen feet apart. Place the ball, which is known as the bacon, in the middle between the two teams.

Give each player of the first team a number, starting with the number one, and do the same for the other team. You will then call out a random number. The two players who were given that number will rush out to try to get the bacon. One of the two players will try to tag the player who grabs the bacon. If a player gets the bacon without being tagged by the other person, that player will bring it back to his or her side and receive a point. If the player is tagged while holding the bacon, then no one receives a point, and the bacon goes back to the middle for the next pair of players to try for.

Participants may play as long as they like, or set a point amount to reach in order to end the game. The team with the most points wins.

2 teams of 3 or more and a leader

Ball (a beach ball works great)

Sticky Famous

Before the players assemble, write the names of famous people on the notes, one person per note. Give everyone a note, cautioning her or him not to look at the name written on it. Then have the players put the notes on their forehead and form a circle. Each person asks the other players in turn questions about the name written on her or his sticky note. Once the asker has gone around the circle once, the turn passes to the next person in the circle. The first person to successfully guess the identity of the person written on her or his note wins the game.

NUMBER OF PLAYERS

4 or more

WHAT YOU'LL NEED

Sticky notes

Pen or marker

Stuff the Sock

Give everyone a sock and a spoon. Have
the candy in the bowl in the center of the
table. When the game starts, players will
have to fill their socks by the spoonful
as fast as they can. The first player to fill
their sock wins the game.

NUMBER OF PLAYERS

2 or more

WHAT YOU'LL NEED

Socks

Spoons

**Small wrapped
candies**

Medium bowl

Tabletop Pyramid

With one minute on the stopwatch, the player must take a stack of thirty-six cups and build a pyramid, starting with a bottom row of eight cups and leading up to one cup at the top. The player must then put the cups back into a single stack before time is up. If the player can complete the task, he or she wins. If no one can stack all thirty-six cups, the person with the largest number of stacked cups wins.

NUMBER OF PLAYERS

2 or more

WHAT YOU'LL NEED

36 plastic cups

Stopwatch

Take a Hike!

Put all the chairs in a circle and have one person (the "middleperson") stand in the center. Have all the other participants take a seat in a chair. The person in the middle makes a statement about her or his interests, ending in the phrase "take a hike."

For example, the person could say, "If you don't like coconut, take a hike," "If you have ever been to New York, take a hike," or "If you have ever run a marathon, take a hike." Whomever this applies to, along with the middleperson, has to get up and find new seats. The player who isn't able to find a seat now becomes the middleperson and must make a statement. This game can go on as long as you like because it's always good for a laugh.

NUMBER OF PLAYERS

4 or more

WHAT YOU'LL NEED

Enough chairs for all but 1 player

Talent Search

You can put this together in person or set it up online by inviting everyone to your preferred virtual hangout, whether that's Google, Zoom, or some other platform. One by one, ask everyone if they have any special talents. It can be anything, like origami, singing, being double-jointed—anything at all. Ask them to then showcase their talent for the next two to three minutes. When everyone has performed, take a vote on who was best.

NUMBER OF PLAYERS

4 or more

WHAT YOU'LL NEED

N/A

Tea Party

Start by taping the tea bag strings to the bill of the hat, one on each side. After a player puts the hat on, set the stopwatch for one minute. When the clock starts, the player will need to swing his or her head in an attempt to get the tea bags to land on the top of the bill. They must stay on top of the bill for three seconds. If someone completes this task, that person wins the challenge.

NUMBER OF PLAYERS

2 or more

WHAT YOU'LL NEED

Tea bags

Duct tape

Baseball cap

Stopwatch

Tennis Balls in the Balance

Begin by placing the wrapping-paper tube in a standing, upright position. Balance the yardstick flat on top of the tube, then start the clock. Two players acting as a team must hang one tennis ball on each end of the yardstick without touching the stick or tube, and can only place one tennis ball on at a time per person.

After making sure each pair of tennis balls is stable, the team can then move on to the next two tennis balls, repeating the same process. If anything falls off or apart, the game is over. If a team gets all the tennis balls on, five on each side, and the whole thing stands for three seconds, that team wins the challenge.

NUMBER OF PLAYERS

2 divided into teams

WHAT YOU'LL NEED

Wrapping-paper tube

Yardstick

10 tennis balls with hooks pushed into them

Stopwatch

Trash Can Basketball

Put trash cans at several distances and heights, giving each one a point value. Players will take turns to try to throw the wadded-up paper in the baskets. They can take as many shots as they want in two minutes. The points are then added up, and the player with the highest score wins.

Truth or Dare

You can play this one in person or gather friends together in an online video conference. When players choose "truth," the person sitting to their right asks a question, which they must answer truthfully in front of the group. Online players can choose a player to answer their question ahead of time. Players can, instead, choose "dare," and the person to their right will dare them to do something, probably something they never imagined doing! If a player decides not to take the dare, he or she drops out of the game. The winner is the last person standing.

NUMBER OF PLAYERS

4 or more

WHAT YOU'LL NEED

N/A

Truth or Manners

During dinner tell everyone certain rules must be observed. If they see someone not adhering to these rules (and the rules should be *very* picky—things like not putting a pinky up when drinking, not wiping your mouth with a napkin after each bite, not putting elbows on the table, etc.), they should call it out. The person breaking the rules is then asked a question by whoever called him or her out. The question can be as personal as you like, and the person must then answer the question truthfully. One person keeps track of how many times each guest is called out. The person who was asked the least amount of questions at the end of dinner wins.

NUMBER OF PLAYERS

2 or more

WHAT YOU'LL NEED

N/A

Try to Guess Celebrity Guests

Write down the name of a popular celebrity of the nineties, or come up with a different common thread, on each of the sheets of paper. As everyone gathers, pin a name on their back so they cannot see who they are. They can ask questions about themselves, but no one can reveal who they are—they must figure it out on their own. The first person who figures out his or her identity is the winner.

NUMBER OF PLAYERS

2 or more

WHAT YOU'LL NEED

Paper

Marker

Safety pins

Turkey Feather Blow

For this game, set the stopwatch for a minute. When it starts ticking down, each player must throw the feather in the air. A player has to keep it in the air by blowing on it. He or she cannot touch it with any body part. If it hits the ground or lands on something before a minute is up, the player is out. If someone can manage to keep the feather in the air, then that person gets a point. Decide how many rounds of feather blowing players should indulge in, and the person with the most points at the end wins the contest.

2 or more

Stopwatch

Turkey feather

Tweezed

A tennis racket is balanced on the end of its handle on a table. You then need to balance a tennis ball on the head of the racket and place a cup under the other side of the racket.

A player is given a pair of tweezers and must pick up a mint and put it through one of the holes of the racket strings and drop it into the cup. The player cannot move the racket or touch it with her or his hands. If the mint doesn't make it into the cup, the player can try again, but if the ball falls off or the racket falls, the player is out.

If someone can get the mint in the cup before one minute is up, she or he gets a point. The person with the most points wins.

NUMBER OF PLAYERS

2 or more

WHAT YOU'LL NEED

Tennis racket

Tennis ball

Cup

Tweezers

Small mints

Stopwatch

Two Truths and a Lie

Everyone gathers in a room, whether that's in person or virtually. Pick someone to start. That person must tell three things about him- or herself, two of which are true and one of which is a lie. Everyone gets to choose which one is the lie. Whoever guesses correctly gets a point. If no one guesses correctly, the person who told the truths and lie gets a point. Decide how many times you want to go around, and at the end the person with the most points wins.

'Ulu Maika

'Ulu Maika is a Hawaiian lawn game.
Pound the two wooden stakes into the
ground about six inches apart. The
players will stand at least twelve feet
back from the stakes. The object of the
game, taking turns, is to roll the stone in
between the two wooden stakes. It seems
simple enough, but this game actually
takes patience and concentration. If all
players get the stone through the stakes
on the same turn, have them go again
until only one is successful.

NUMBER OF PLAYERS

2 or more

WHAT YOU'LL NEED

**2 wooden stakes that
can be pounded into
the ground (like cro-
quet stakes)**

Medium-sized stone

Uphill Battle

To get this game ready, you will need to place the books under two legs of a table, giving the table a minor slant. Players must gather three of the marbles onto the spoon and hold them on the table. When the timer starts, players let the marbles go and keep them from going off the table by tapping them with the spoon. Players can only use one hand to hold the spoon, and no other part of them is to make contact with anything. If a player can keep the marbles from rolling off for one minute, he or she gets a point. Whoever has the most points when everyone has gone three times wins the game.

NUMBER OF PLAYERS

3 or more

WHAT YOU'LL NEED

2 phone books or thick books

Marbles

Wooden spoon

Stopwatch

Volcano

This one is a bit of a science experiment. It should definitely be done outside. Players will need to kneel on a chair or any elevated surface. Place the two-liter bottle below the player and have the player hold the Mentos in his or her hand, raised overhead. If the player can drop the mint into the soda in less than a minute and cause a volcanic eruption, he or she wins! (Be sure to surround the soda bottle with newspapers or something else absorbent, or better yet, do it outside; this can get kind of messy!)

NUMBER OF PLAYERS

4 or more

WHAT YOU'LL NEED

2-liter bottle of diet cola

Mentos mints

Stopwatch

Volleyball Splash

Have the players stand on opposite sides of the pool facing one another. The first person will pick up the wet sponge and serve it, like a volleyball, to the other player(s). The object of the game is to keep the sponge in the air. If it lands on the ground, the player(s) who did not touch the sponge last get(s) a point. If it lands in the pool, the last one to touch it loses a point. The first player to get ten points is the winner.

Water Balloon Hunt

It's best to play this game outside. Hide the water balloons all over the area in which the game will be played. Separate the players into two teams, and assign each team a bucket and a home station. Once the game starts, each team has five minutes to find as many water balloons as possible and put them in their bucket. Once the five minutes are up, tally the balloons to see who won, and then the teams can launch an attack on each other with their collected balloons! Due to the use of balloons, make sure no one is allergic to latex before the game.

NUMBER OF PLAYERS

4 or more divided into 2 teams

WHAT YOU'LL NEED

Lots of latex water balloons (at least a couple dozen), filled up in advance

A bucket for each team

Stopwatch

Water Balloon Scramble

Separate the players into two teams. Have each player tie a "belt" around his or her waist made from the cotton twine or yarn. Each team should have its own color of twine or yarn.

Tie one filled water balloon or more around each player's waist using the cotton twine or yarn, making sure each player has the same number of balloons. Set the stopwatch for two minutes. Have the teams stand opposite each other. When someone yells, "Go," each team will try to pop all the balloons on the belts of the opposite team with their hands or any other body part. After two minutes, have the players return to their sides. Do a balloon count, and the team with the most remaining balloons is the winner. Due to the use of balloons, make sure no one is allergic to latex before the game.

4 or more divided into 2 teams

Cotton twine or yarn (in 2 different colors)

At least 1 prefilled latex water balloon per player (though you can have more)

Stopwatch

Watermelon Ninja

Place the watermelon with the cut side toward the player. The player, from three feet away, has one minute to flick as many of the cards sideways so they stick in the watermelon. A player receives one point for every card that is stuck. If any of the cards are knocked out, they're deducted from the score at the end of the minute. The player with the highest score wins.

2 or more

Watermelon cut in half

Standard deck of 52 playing cards

Stopwatch

What's That Line?

You can decide if you want to make this specific to a genre or time era, depending on whom you're playing with. You can also play in person or set up a virtual hangout online to gather friends from everywhere. Cue up a song and have a player stand up to sing. Play the song, and the person must sing along. Pause the song whenever you like, and the player must finish the next line of the song in order to move on to the next round. Continue with rounds until two people are left to compete. They will challenge each other until someone doesn't know the line. The winner is then crowned.

2 or more

Music and player

APPENDIX:

Games by Type

ART AND CREATIVITY GAMES

Artist's Paint-and-Pass

Bridge Master

Commercial Life

Flip-a-Song Karaoke

Flip-Book Frenzy

Hungry Puzzler

Mad Lib Story

Masquerade

Model Drawing

Mug Shots

Talent Search

COMPETITION GAMES

Apple on a String

Back-to-Back Sumo

Ball Battle

Candy Hunt

Crystal Clear Game

Egg Drop

Flour Game

Following the Leader

Going on a Picnic

Guess That Tune

Horse

Movie and Show Trivia

Name the Celebrity

Name the Difference

Office Chair Catapult

Office Supply Fishing

Ostrich Dance

Sneak a Peek

Spoon Brainteaser

Stuff the Sock

Trash Can Basketball

DECADE PARTY GAMES

1920s Dance-Off

Dress-and-Dash Relay

Pin the Mullet on the Dude

Try to Guess Celebrity Guests

What's That Line?

DINNER PARTY GAMES

All Thumbs

Celebrity Dinner Theater

Celebrity Hunt

Check Your Pockets

Cheese Taste-Off

Freeze

Grand Tour

Ingredients Throw-Down

Monkey See, Monkey Do

Most Likely To...

Murder Mystery Game

Musical Teacups

Nickname Name Tag

Our Future and Then...

Psychologist

Room Recall

Rorschach Test

Shoes Up

Song Charades

Soul Mate

Spice Savvy

Spoons

Sticky Famous

Two Truths and a Lie

GROUP GAMES	MINUTE-TO-WIN GAMES
ABC Roundup	Bobble Head
Ask Me About...	Caddy Stack
Back-to-Back	Clipboard Tennis
Balloon Keep-Away	Cookie Face
Cups and Downs	Defy Gravity
Don't Look Back	Drop, Sink, and Clink
Dress-Off	Gum Bobbing
Feed Me!	Head Pendulum
Fishbowl	Leap Spoon
How's Yours?	Minute-to-Win-It Iron Man
Hurry! Hurry! Make the List	Mummy Wrap
Improv in a Bag	Noodling Around
Job Charades	Paper Scraper
Movie Trivia	Stack Me
Musical Balance	Tabletop Pyramid
On Your Mark, Get Set, Draw!	Tea Party
Plastic Wrap	Tennis Balls in the Balance
Prediction Bingo	Turkey Feather Blow
Presentation Memory	Tweezed
Shakedown	Uphill Battle
Take a Hike!	Volcano

Back-to-Back Balloon Dash

Balloon Waddle

Balloon Word Scramble

Bucket Guard

Candy Relay

Carrot Toss

Chalky Target

Egg Head Spin-and-Attack

Egg Roller Relay

Fragile-Package Toss

Homemade Ball Toss

Hoop Toss

Jug Master

Pass the Mango

Puff Ball Fight

Slippery Dash

Steal the Bacon

'Ulu Maika

Volleyball Splash

Water Balloon Hunt

Water Balloon Scramble

Watermelon Ninja

Blind Man's Treasure

Hide-and-Seek

Household Scavenger Hunt

Never Have I Ever

Truth or Dare

Truth or Manners

Index

1920s Dance-Off, 15

ABC Roundup, 17
All Thumbs, 18
Apple on a String, 19
Art games
    Artist's Paint-and-Pass, 20
    Bridge Master, 35
    Commercial Life, 49
    Flip-a-Song Karaoke, 66
    Flip-Book Frenzy, 67
    Hungry Puzzler, 85
    Mad Lib Story, 93
    Masquerade, 95
    Model Drawing, 97
    Mug Shots, 102
    On Your Mark, Get Set, Draw!, 120
    Room Recall, 133
    Talent Search, 154
Artist's Paint-and-Pass, 20
Ask Me About..., 22

Back-to-Back, 23
Back-to-Back Balloon Dash, 25
Back-to-Back Sumo, 26
Bacon, Steal the, 148
Balance, Musical, 108
Balance, Tennis Balls, 157
Ball Battle, 27
Ball games
    Ball Battle, 27
    Bucket Guard, 36

Caddy Stack, 38
Clipboard Tennis, 48
Don't Look Back, 54
Head Pendulum, 77
Homemade Ball Toss, 80
Horse, 82
Jug Master, 91
Plastic Wrap, 128
Puff Ball Fight, 132
Shakedown, 135
Steal the Bacon, 148
Tennis Balls in the Balance, 157
Trash Can Basketball, 158
Tweezed, 164
Volleyball Splash, 169
Balloon games
    Back-to-Back Balloon Dash, 25
    Balloon Keep-Away, 28
    Balloon Waddle, 29
    Balloon Word Scramble, 30
    Bucket Guard, 36
    Defy Gravity, 53
    Egg Head Spin-and-Attack, 61
    Fragile-Package Toss, 71
    Jug Master, 91
    Water Balloon Hunt, 170
    Water Balloon Scramble, 171
Balloon Hunt, 170
Balloon Keep-Away, 28
Balloon Scramble, 171
Balloon Waddle, 29
Balloon Word Scramble, 30

Basket/bucket games
   Bucket Guard, 36
   Chalky Target, 45
   Clipboard Tennis, 48
   Horse, 82
   Slippery Dash, 138
   Trash Can Basketball, 158
   Water Balloon Hunt, 170
Battle, Ball, 27
Battle, Uphill, 167
Bingo, Prediction, 129
Blind Man's Treasure, 32
Bobbing, Gum, 76
Bobble Head, 33
Brainteaser, Spoon, 144
Bridge Master, 35
Bucket Guard, 36
Building/stacking games
   Bridge Master, 35
   Caddy Stack, 38
   Minute-to-Win-It Iron Man, 96
   Paper Scraper, 123
   Sneak a Peek, 139
   Stack Me, 147
   Tabletop Pyramid, 152

Caddy Stack, 38
Candy Hunt, 39
Candy Relay, 40
Carrot Toss, 41
Catapult, Office Chair, 117
Celebrity Dinner Theater, 42

Celebrity Guests, Try to Guess, 161
Celebrity Hunt, 43
Celebrity, Name the, 111
Chalky Target, 45
Charades
   Job Charades, 89
   Monkey See, Monkey Do, 98
   Song Charades, 140
Check Your Pockets, 46
Cheese Taste-Off, 47
Clipboard Tennis, 48
Clothing/mask games
   Dress-and-Dash Relay, 56
   Dress-Off, 57
   Masquerade, 95
   Shoes Up, 137
   Stuff the Sock, 150
Coin games
   Drop, Sink, and Clink, 59
   Never Have I Ever, 113
Commercial Life, 49
Competition games. *See also*
   Minute-to-win games
   1920s Dance-Off, 15
   Apple on a String, 19
   Back-to-Back Balloon Dash, 25
   Back-to-Back Sumo, 26
   Ball Battle, 27
   Balloon Waddle, 29
   Candy Hunt, 39
   Candy Relay, 40
   Chalky Target, 45

Competition games—*continued*
    Cheese Taste-Off, 47
    Crystal Clear Game, 51
    Dress-and-Dash Relay, 56
    Egg Drop, 60
    Egg Roller Relay, 62
    Flour Game, 69
    Following the Leader, 70
    Going on a Picnic, 73
    Guess That Tune, 75
    Horse, 82
    Movie and Show Trivia, 100
    Movie Trivia, 101
    Name the Celebrity, 111
    Name the Difference, 112
    Office Chair Catapult, 117
    Office Supply Fishing, 118
    Ostrich Dance, 121
    Pass the Mango, 125
    Slippery Dash, 138
    Sneak a Peek, 139
    Spoon Brainteaser, 144
    Stuff the Sock, 150
    Trash Can Basketball, 158
    Volleyball Splash, 169
    Water Balloon Scramble, 171
    What's That Line?, 174
Cookie Face, 50
Creativity games
    Artist's Paint-and-Pass, 20
    Bridge Master, 35
    Commercial Life, 49
    Flip-a-Song Karaoke, 66

    Flip-Book Frenzy, 67
    Hungry Puzzler, 85
    Improv in a Bag, 87
    Ingredients Throw-Down, 88
    Mad Lib Story, 93
    Masquerade, 95
    Model Drawing, 97
    Mug Shots, 102
    On Your Mark, Get Set, Draw!, 120
    Room Recall, 133
    Talent Search, 154
Crystal Clear Game, 51
Cups and Downs, 52

Dance-Off, 1920s, 15
Dance, Ostrich, 121
Dashes/races. *See also* Relay games
    Back-to-Back Balloon Dash, 25
    Balloon Waddle, 29
    Dress-and-Dash Relay, 56
    Pass the Mango, 125
    Slippery Dash, 138
Decade party games. *See also* Party games
    1920s Dance-Off, 15
    Dress-and-Dash Relay, 56
    Pin the Mullet on the Dude, 126
    Try to Guess Celebrity Guests, 161
    What's That Line?, 174

BORED GAMES

Defy Gravity, 53
Difference, Name the, 112
Dinner party games. *See also*
   Party games
   All Thumbs, 18
   Celebrity Dinner Theater, 42
   Celebrity Hunt, 43
   Check Your Pockets, 46
   Cheese Taste-Off, 47
   Freeze, 72
   Grand Tour, 74
   Ingredients Throw-Down, 88
   Monkey See, Monkey Do, 98
   Most Likely To..., 99
   Murder Mystery Game, 106–7
   Musical Teacups, 110
   Nickname Name Tag, 115
   Our Future and Then..., 122
   Psychologist, 131
   Room Recall, 133
   Rorschach Test, 134
   Shoes Up, 137
   Song Charades, 140
   Soul Mate, 141
   Spice Savvy, 142
   Spoons, 145
   Sticky Famous, 149
   Two Truths and a Lie, 165
Don't Look Back, 54
Drawing, Model, 97
Dress-and-Dash Relay, 56
Dress-Off, 57
Drop, Sink, and Clink, 59

Egg Drop, 60
Egg games
   Bridge Master, 35
   Egg Drop, 60
   Egg Head Spin-and-Attack,
      61
   Egg Roller Relay, 62
Egg Head Spin-and-Attack, 61
Egg Roller Relay, 62

Famous, Sticky, 149
Feather Blow, Turkey, 162
Feed Me!, 64
Fight, Puff Ball, 132
Fishbowl/fishing games
   Drop, Sink, and Clink, 59
   Fishbowl, 65
   Office Supply Fishing, 118
Flip-a-Song Karaoke, 66
Flip-Book Frenzy, 67
Flour Game, 69
Following the Leader, 70
Food games
   Apple on a String, 19
   Candy Hunt, 39
   Candy Relay, 40
   Carrot Toss, 41
   Cheese Taste-Off, 47
   Cookie Face, 50
   Egg Drop, 60
   Egg Roller Relay, 62
   Feed Me!, 64
   Flour Game, 69

Food games—*continued*
   Ingredients Throw-Down, 88
   Noodling Around, 116
   Pass the Mango, 125
   Spice Savvy, 142
   Stuff the Sock, 150
   Truth or Manners, 160
Fragile-Package Toss, 71
Freeze, 72

Going on a Picnic, 73
Grand Tour, 74
Gravity, Defy, 53
Group games. *See also*
   Competition games; Party
   games
   1920s Dance-Off, 15
   ABC Roundup, 17
   All Thumbs, 18
   Ask Me About…, 22
   Back-to-Back, 23
   Balloon Keep-Away, 28
   Balloon Word Scramble, 30
   Blind Man's Treasure, 32
   Bucket Guard, 36
   Carrot Toss, 41
   Chalky Target, 45
   Check Your Pockets, 46
   Clipboard Tennis, 48
   Commercial Life, 49
   Cups and Downs, 52
   Don't Look Back, 54
   Dress-Off, 57

Egg Drop, 60
Egg Roller Relay, 62
Feed Me!, 64
Fishbowl, 65
Flip-a-Song Karaoke, 66
Flip-Book Frenzy, 67
Following the Leader, 70
Fragile-Package Toss, 71
Freeze, 72
Going on a Picnic, 73
Grand Tour, 74
Hide-and-Seek, 78
How's Yours?, 84
Hungry Puzzler, 85
Hurry! Hurry! Make the List,
   86
Improv in a Bag, 87
Ingredients Throw-Down, 88
Job Charades, 89
Jug Master, 91
Mad Lib Story, 93
Masquerade, 95
Monkey See, Monkey Do, 98
Most Likely To…, 99
Movie and Show Trivia, 100
Movie Trivia, 101
Mug Shots, 102
Mummy Wrap, 105
Murder Mystery Game, 106–7
Musical Balance, 108
Musical Teacups, 110
On Your Mark, Get Set, Draw!,
   120

Pass the Mango, 125
Plastic Wrap, 128
Prediction Bingo, 129
Presentation Memory, 130
Puff Ball Fight, 132
Shakedown, 135
Sneak a Peek, 139
Song Charades, 140
Stack Me, 147
Steal the Bacon, 148
Sticky Famous, 149
Take a Hike!, 153
Talent Search, 154
Truth or Dare, 159
Water Balloon Hunt, 170
Water Balloon Scramble, 171
Guess That Tune, 75
Guessing games
    Ask Me About..., 22
    Celebrity Dinner Theater, 42
    Cheese Taste-Off, 47
    Fishbowl, 65
    Guess That Tune, 75
    How's Yours?, 84
    Job Charades, 89
    Monkey See, Monkey Do, 98
    Movie and Show Trivia, 100
    Movie Trivia, 101
    Murder Mystery Game, 106–7
    Name the Celebrity, 111
    On Your Mark, Get Set, Draw!,
        120
    Psychologist, 131

Rorschach Test, 134
Song Charades, 140
Soul Mate, 141
Spoon Brainteaser, 144
Sticky Famous, 149
Try to Guess Celebrity Guests,
    161
Two Truths and a Lie, 165
What's That Line?, 174
Gum Bobbing, 76

Head Pendulum, 77
Hide-and-Seek, 78
Hike, Take a, 153
Homemade Ball Toss, 80
Hoop Toss, 81
Horse, 82
Household Scavenger Hunt, 83
How's Yours?, 84
Hungry Puzzler, 85
Hunting games
    Blind Man's Treasure, 32
    Candy Hunt, 39
    Celebrity Hunt, 43
    Hide-and-Seek, 78
    Household Scavenger Hunt,
        83
    Water Balloon Hunt, 170
Hurry! Hurry! Make the List, 86

Improv in a Bag, 87
Ingredients Throw-Down, 88
Iron Man, Minute-to-Win-It, 96

Job Charades, 89
Jug Master, 91

Karaoke, Flip-a-Song, 66
Keep-Away, Balloon, 28

Leader, Following the, 70
Leap Spoon, 92

Mad Lib Story, 93
Mango, Pass the, 125
Masquerade, 95
Memory games
    Going on a Picnic, 73
    Grand Tour, 74
    Name the Difference, 112
    Presentation Memory, 130
    Room Recall, 133
Minute-to-win games
    Blind Man's Treasure, 32
    Bobble Head, 33
    Caddy Stack, 38
    Clipboard Tennis, 48
    Cookie Face, 50
    Cups and Downs, 52
    Defy Gravity, 53
    Drop, Sink, and Clink, 59
    Fishbowl, 65
    Gum Bobbing, 76
    Head Pendulum, 77
    Leap Spoon, 92
    Minute-to-Win-It Iron Man,
        96

Mummy Wrap, 105
Noodling Around, 116
Paper Scraper, 123
Plastic Wrap, 128
Shakedown, 135
Stack Me, 147
Tabletop Pyramid, 152
Tea Party, 155
Tennis Balls in the Balance,
    157
Turkey Feather Blow, 162
Tweezed, 164
Uphill Battle, 167
Volcano, 168
Watermelon Ninja, 173
Minute-to-Win-It Iron Man, 96
Model Drawing, 97
Monkey See, Monkey Do, 98
Most Likely To..., 99
Movie and Show Trivia, 100
Movie Trivia, 101
Mug Shots, 102
Mullet, Pin on the Dude, 126
Mummy Wrap, 105
Murder Mystery Game, 106–7
Musical Balance, 108
Musical games
    1920s Dance-Off, 15
    Dress-Off, 57
    Flip-a-Song Karaoke, 66
    Guess That Tune, 75
    Musical Balance, 108
    Musical Teacups, 110

BORED GAMES

Song Charades, 140
What's That Line?, 174
Musical Teacups, 110

Name tag games
    Ask Me About..., 22
    Nickname Name Tag, 115
Name the Celebrity, 111
Name the Difference, 112
Never Have I Ever, 113
Nickname Name Tag, 115
Ninja, Watermelon, 173
Noodling Around, 116

Office Chair Catapult, 117
Office Supply Fishing, 118
On Your Mark, Get Set, Draw!,
    120
Ostrich Dance, 121
Our Future and Then..., 122
Outdoor games. *See also*
    Summer games
    Back-to-Back Balloon Dash, 25
    Balloon Waddle, 29
    Bucket Guard, 36
    Chalky Target, 45
    Egg Head Spin-and-Attack, 61
    Fragile-Package Toss, 71
    Head Pendulum, 77
    Homemade Ball Toss, 80
    Hoop Toss, 81
    Horse, 82
    Jug Master, 91

Puff Ball Fight, 132
Slippery Dash, 138
Steal the Bacon, 148
'Ulu Maika, 166
Volcano, 168
Volleyball Splash, 169
Water Balloon Hunt, 170
Water Balloon Scramble, 171

Package Toss, Fragile, 71
Paint-and-Pass, Artist's, 20
Paper Scraper, 123
Party games. *See also* Group
    games
    1920s Dance-Off, 15
    All Thumbs, 18
    Celebrity Dinner Theater, 42
    Celebrity Hunt, 43
    Check Your Pockets, 46
    Cheese Taste-Off, 47
    Dress-and-Dash Relay, 56
    Freeze, 72
    Grand Tour, 74
    Ingredients Throw-Down, 88
    Monkey See, Monkey Do, 98
    Most Likely To..., 99
    Murder Mystery Game, 106–7
    Musical Balance, 108
    Musical Teacups, 110
    Nickname Name Tag, 115
    Our Future and Then..., 122
    Pin the Mullet on the Dude,
        126

Party games—*continued*
 Psychologist, 131
 Room Recall, 133
 Rorschach Test, 134
 Shoes Up, 137
 Song Charades, 140
 Soul Mate, 141
 Spice Savvy, 142
 Spoons, 145
 Sticky Famous, 149
 Tea Party, 155
 Try to Guess Celebrity Guests,
  161
 Two Truths and a Lie, 165
 What's That Line?, 174
Pass the Mango, 125
Peek, Sneak a, 139
Pendulum, Head, 77
Picnic, Going on, 73
Pin the Mullet on the Dude, 126
Plastic Wrap, 128
Pockets, Check Your, 46
Prediction Bingo, 129
Presentation Memory, 130
Psychologist, 131
Puff Ball Fight, 132
Puzzler, Hungry, 85
Pyramid, Tabletop, 152

Relay games. *See also* Dashes/
 races
 Candy Relay, 40
 Dress-and-Dash Relay, 56

 Egg Roller Relay, 62
Room Recall, 133
Rorschach Test, 134

Scavenger hunt games
 Blind Man's Treasure, 32
 Hide-and-Seek, 78
 Household Scavenger Hunt,
  83
Scramble, Balloon Word, 30
Scramble, Water Balloon, 171
Shakedown, 135
Shoes Up, 137
Slippery Dash, 138
Sneak a Peek, 139
Sock, Stuff the, 150
Song Charades, 140
Soul Mate, 141
Spice Savvy, 142
Spin-and-Attack, Egg Head, 61
Splash, Volleyball, 169
Spoon Brainteaser, 144
Spoon games
 Feed Me!, 64
 Leap Spoon, 92
 Spoon Brainteaser, 144
 Spoons, 145
 Stuff the Sock, 150
 Uphill Battle, 167
Spoons, 145
Stack Me, 147
Stacking games
 Caddy Stack, 38

Minute-to-Win-It Iron Man, 96
Stack Me, 147
Tabletop Pyramid, 152
Steal the Bacon, 148
Sticky Famous, 149
Storytelling games
Flip-Book Frenzy, 67
Mad Lib Story, 93
Our Future and Then..., 122
String/yarn games
Apple on a String, 19
Balloon Keep-Away, 28
Office Supply Fishing, 118
Shakedown, 135
Tea Party, 155
Water Balloon Scramble, 171
Stuff the Sock, 150
Summer games. *See also*
Outdoor games
Back-to-Back Balloon Dash, 25
Balloon Waddle, 29
Balloon Word Scramble, 30
Bucket Guard, 36
Candy Relay, 40
Carrot Toss, 41
Chalky Target, 45
Egg Head Spin-and-Attack, 61
Egg Roller Relay, 62
Fragile-Package Toss, 71
Homemade Ball Toss, 80
Hoop Toss, 81
Jug Master, 91
Pass the Mango, 125

Puff Ball Fight, 132
Slippery Dash, 138
Steal the Bacon, 148
'Ulu Maika, 166
Volleyball Splash, 169
Water Balloon Hunt, 170
Water Balloon Scramble, 171
Watermelon Ninja, 173
Sumo, Back-to-Back, 26

Tabletop Pyramid, 152
Take a Hike!, 153
Talent Search, 154
Target, Chalky, 45
Taste-Off, Cheese, 47
Tea Party, 155
Teacups, Musical, 110
Tennis Balls in the Balance, 157
Tennis, Clipboard, 48
Theme parties
1920s Dance-Off, 15
Masquerade, 95
Murder Mystery Game, 106–7
Pin the Mullet on the Dude, 126
Tossing/throwing games
Bucket Guard, 36
Carrot Toss, 41
Chalky Target, 45
Clipboard Tennis, 48
Don't Look Back, 54
Egg Head Spin-and-Attack, 61
Fragile-Package Toss, 71

Tossing/throwing games
—*continued*
  Homemade Ball Toss, 80
  Hoop Toss, 81
  Horse, 82
  Jug Master, 91
  Trash Can Basketball, 158
Tour, Grand, 74
Trash Can Basketball, 158
Treasure hunt games
  Blind Man's Treasure, 32
  Hide-and-Seek, 78
  Household Scavenger Hunt, 83
Trivia games
  Guess That Tune, 75
  Movie and Show Trivia, 100
  Movie Trivia, 101
  Name the Celebrity, 111
Truth-or-dare games
  Never Have I Ever, 113
  Truth or Dare, 159
  Truth or Manners, 160
  Two Truths and a Lie, 165
Try to Guess Celebrity Guests, 161
Turkey Feather Blow, 162
Tweezed, 164
Two Truths and a Lie, 165

'Ulu Maika, 166
Uphill Battle, 167

Volcano, 168
Volleyball Splash, 169

Water balloon games
  Back-to-Back Balloon Dash, 25
  Bucket Guard, 36
  Egg Head Spin-and-Attack, 61
  Fragile-Package Toss, 71
  Jug Master, 91
  Water Balloon Hunt, 170
  Water Balloon Scramble, 171
Water Balloon Hunt, 170
Water Balloon Scramble, 171
Watermelon Ninja, 173
What's That Line?, 174
Word/letter games
  ABC Roundup, 17
  Balloon Word Scramble, 30
  Celebrity Hunt, 43
  Going on a Picnic, 73
  Horse, 82
  How's Yours?, 84
  Mad Lib Story, 93
  Nickname Name Tag, 115
  Ostrich Dance, 121
  Spoons, 145
Word Scramble, Balloon, 30
Wrap, Mummy, 105
Wrap, Plastic, 128